Frame and Fortune

STEVE DAVIS

Frame and Fortune

As told to Brian Radford

Arthur Barker Limited London
A SUBSIDIARY OF WEIDENFELD (PUBLISHERS) LIMITED

BY THE SAME AUTHOR:

Steve Davis: Snooker Champion

Published in Great Britain by
Arthur Barker Ltd
91 Clapham High Street
London SW4 7TA

ISBN 0 213 16840 5

Printed in Great Britain by
Butler & Tanner Ltd, Frome and London

Contents

Acknowledgements

The photographs in this book are reproduced by kind permission of the following: BBC Television, Central Television, Coral Racing Ltd, Courage Breweries Ltd, *Daily Mail*, *Daily Star*, Express Newspapers Ltd, Mel Figures, *Lancashire Evening Post*, Jim Latham, Leisure Industries, London Weekend Television, Dave Muscroft, *Oldham Chronicle*, *Staffordshire Sentinel*. The diagrams are by Heather Sherratt.

This book is dedicated to
snooker supporters all over the world

I

King of the Castle

With the World Cup resting in my arms, and with the experience of the past two weeks still buzzing around in my head, I hardly slept a wink. The silver pot was too large to push under the bed, so I took it under the sheets with me. Even then, several hours on, I still found it hard to believe that I was waking up on 20 April 1981, as the world's new professional snooker champion.

My first morning as top dog started with a bang. The bedroom door swung open and I was mobbed by a pack of Press photographers still competing frantically for that final off-beat picture of me and the trophy. The endless merry-go-round of success had already begun. The celebratory bacon sandwiches and orange juice had to wait!

As time went by, the porter delivered the daily papers and the big headlines, and even bigger pictures, left me in no doubt that I really was the king of the castle. It was all very strange, but the full impact of becoming world champion hadn't actually sunk in. Somehow, I needed to see it in print. To confirm that I had really beaten Doug Mountjoy eighteen games to twelve at the packed Crucible Theatre in Sheffield.

Eventually, the photographers ran out of film, the reporters ran out of ink – and I ran out of the Grosvenor Hotel and pointed my red

Rover down the M1, the World Cup sitting alongside me in the passenger's seat.

My two weeks in Sheffield had been a major assignment. Now the job was done and, just like Mission Impossible, I was 'moving on'. It would have been nice to return home to a hero's welcome, just like the one I had seen at Llanelli two years earlier when Terry Griffiths was given a rapturous reception. Instead, I was about to begin the most hectic year of my life. Even then I knew it would be a full month before I could get home and sleep in my own bed!

After leaving Sheffield I stopped at a motorway café. A few kids came up and asked for my autograph and wanted to know 'is that really the World Cup?' lying on the seat.

I said, 'Yeh! Great, isn't it?' I was as excited as they were.

Chatteris was my first stop. A small, picturesque village in Cambridgeshire. My good friend Snowy Salisbury, a top-class county billiards player, had invited me to stay with him while playing my first exhibition match as world champion at the Peterborough Football Club.

Snowy's house stands in its own grounds, sheltered by a line of tall trees at the end of a long lane. It is far out in the country. As I reached the end of the lane, I stopped the car and got out. There was almost total silence. Only the occasional twitter of a bird on a branch gave any indication of life on Earth. What a contrast to all the noise and bustle I had experienced back at the Crucible. It felt a million miles away. For once, I was alone with my thoughts.

Snowy inevitably murdered me in a game of billiards before his wife Kay fattened me up with a massive fillet steak and heaps and heaps of veg. I must have lost half a stone during the championships and, seeing that I have to run around to get wet in the shower, I welcomed the chance to eat properly for the first time in two weeks, and I reckon I put the whole lot back in one go before leaving the table.

To reach the Posh Club in Peterborough, Snowy kindly pulled out his glistening Rolls-Royce and offered to drive me there.

'Only a Rolls-Royce will do for a Rolls-Royce snooker player,' he said, and insisted that I sat on the bonnet, holding the trophy in my lap, while he played David Bailey.

Later that evening I walked into the Posh Club with the World Cup shining in my hands and received a tremendous welcome. The standing ovation brought a lump to my throat, and after all that emotion, I suppose it was inevitable that I wouldn't pot a ball. Not that the audience complained. One or two even cheered when I chalked the cue! They seemed pleased just to see me. Then one chap explained that Peterborough crowds were used to seeing players shoot wide from two feet every Saturday afternoon.

A little disappointed with my handiwork, I decided to give my footwork a try and was lured into a disco across the road – and stepped straight into another disaster. The place was fitted out with a close-circuit television system and as soon as I stood up the cameras were focused on my feet. After two weeks of being under the microscope at something I could do, I was now facing even more cameras while attempting something I couldn't do. The pressure was greater than at the Crucible!

Many years ago, I decided that I should learn to disco-dance as I didn't want to look a complete idiot on the floor. I practised for hours in front of a long mirror until I mastered a few steps and was happy with myself. I am far from brilliant, but I can at least move in time with the music.

Tony Meo is snooker's disco king. But even he was put in his place one night in Newcastle. Tony had been on the floor for quite some time, dancing away and enjoying himself, when a young girl he had never seen before, went out and joined him. She was fantastic. Backflips, somersaults, pirouettes – you name it, she did it. She made Tony look a novice. With the spotlight on them all the time, Tony eventually held out his hands and pleaded, 'Tell me! Tell me! What have I done to deserve all this?' And the girl confessed that she was a professional dancer!

I slept at Snowy's after my disco fiasco and found it a pleasure to wake up next morning. I was still gloating. Still smug.

Newspapers continued to report every move I made, and no matter where I went, I was mobbed for autographs. It must be said that one or two players are not always at their best when asked for them. I remember signing a piece of paper for an oldish woman in Manchester while trying to carry on a conversation with my manager Barry Hearn. She seemed to think I was being rude and said, 'This autograph is for my son. Personally, I think your head is too big for your shoulders.' I simply said, 'Thanks, love,' and smiled.

On the lighter side, I remember a queue forming for my autograph on a visit to Newcastle and a man came up and said, 'Who are you, then? I've been working in Germany and you're new to me.'

'I'm a top pianist,' I replied (well, I can dream, can't I?). 'You don't see me on television because I do a lot of backing for the big groups.'

He was hooked on every word. He pushed an envelope into my hand and said, 'In that case, I must have your signature. My son will be so pleased.'

Once in the Devon fishing village of Teignmouth, I was waiting to board a boat with Barry when a woman came up and asked for my autograph. As I was writing it, she said, nastily, 'Actually, I prefer Hurricane Higgins to you!'

Barry thought she had a damned cheek and offered to give her Alex's autograph instead. She fell for it. He took the paper, turned it over, and marked an 'X'.

The most fascinating autograph request I've ever received came from a man who collects signatures of 'famous' people on old ten-bob notes. He has two hundred of them, including one of Muhammad Ali. I've obviously signed many plastered arms and legs, but only rarely have I signed a leg above the knee! However, I did once sign a pair of my underpants for the daughter of a friend to take to school as a dare.

When my plimsolls wore thin, I went to a shop in Sheffield for a new pair. I didn't want to take the old ones away with me, so I asked the girl assistant if she could drop them in a bin.

'Could you please sign them first?' she said. When someone is asked to sign his tatty old plimsolls, I think he is entitled to assume that he really has arrived!

On my second day as world champion, I attended a sales marketing luncheon, a very relaxed affair, with a few games of snooker thrown in. A fair amount of drink was consumed by some of the staff and their guests, which set the scene for a lively party atmosphere. I played Mark Wildman, and the referee, who was picked from the audience, was so drunk that we allowed him to stay in his chair. But even that didn't help. He kept slipping out, on to the carpet, and I kept tripping over his legs. In the end, he slid right out of his seat and fell fast asleep on the floor – and we left him there.

With everyone in such good spirits, Mark and I secretly decided to swap the cue-ball for a trick one which I always carry with me. It is weighted inside, like the woods they use at bowls. So no matter where you strike this ball, it will go shooting off course and finish up in all sorts of odd places. Two guests volunteered to play Mark and me in a game of doubles, and they were so badly drunk that we went right through the frame without either of them realising the white ball was 'bent'.

Once at my local workingmen's club, Dad and I switched the white ball for a giggle, and two men, who were stone cold sober, and regular players, didn't suspect for a second that something was wrong, despite seeing it whizzing around at crazy angles. They truly believed they were still using the correct ball, which suggests they saw the cue-ball only when it was stationary. This again emphasises the wide gulf between the amateur who plays regularly, and the professional, who would notice something was wrong with the ball on his very first shot.

It was while playing billiards at Snowy's home that I decided to take a break from practising snooker over the coming few weeks and to practise billiards instead. A change is as good as a rest, I thought, although billiards, of course, wasn't a complete change. I still had to cue correctly. To start practising snooker so soon after the pressure-fortnight in Sheffield would have been soul-destroying. It was the last thing I wanted to do. Try eating beans on toast for a fortnight, morning, noon and night, and you'll begin to know what I mean. The sight of more and more snooker balls at that stage could only have put me off. My mind needed a rest, and billiards was the obvious and perfect alternative.

The game was not entirely new to me. Over the years, billiards has helped me enormously with my snooker, especially in mastering the finer points of cue-ball control. My father and I haven't always seen eye-to-eye on the value of billiards practice. For a long time after the world championships he worried a great deal that I wasn't putting in enough snooker practice. He believed my form would suffer. He would get awfully uptight about it, and make sarcastic remarks like 'I see in the papers that you're a snooker player, Steve. . . .'

Deep down, my enthusiasm for snooker is as strong as it has ever been, although I believe there are better ways to practice than just going through the motions of playing a game. Playing snooker, and playing it well, is all that matters to me. So many players have either become too big for their boots and think they don't need to practise any more, or become lazy and neglect their practise, that Dad might have secretly feared that I was about to follow in their footsteps. Well, in no way will that happen. Instead, I prefer to think that their mistakes have helped to widen my education. A player should try to build up to his peak before a tournament in the same way as a professional boxer prepares for a title fight. Having said that, we all know it is impossible for any sportsman to remain at his peak all the year round.

I believe the duty of a good champion is to defend all his major titles successfully, and then go out and win as many new ones as he can. The immortal Joe Davis was world champion for twenty years. That alone, I suppose, might be a worthwhile target for me.

Hardly a day goes by now without someone, somewhere, attempting to compare me with the great Joe. One or two good judges who had the rare chance of seeing us both, have been kind enough to say that I would have beaten the mighty man. I would like to have played Joe. He would have brought the best out of me. He would have improved my game. Sometimes I need the push of a strong challenge to draw on my extreme resources.

Similar comparisons have been made between Rocky Marciano and Muhammad Ali. Facts have been fed into computers, but results on this basis alone can never be conclusive. Computers might be capable of assessing a mass of complex statistics, but no machine in the world can tell how each person feels on the night or how he reacts under pressure. There is no question that in snooker, in particular, a player's mental attitude towards a match can be just as important as the skill he produces.

I reckon no one can argue that winning major titles in Joe's time was a lot easier than winning them now. There were fewer tournaments, less pressure and very little in the way of commitments as we know them today. Don't think I'm devaluing Joe's enormous achievements, for I'm not. The record-books speak for themselves.

I met Joe just once, briefly in a gents' toilet during an interval in a match at Drury Lane in London. We never spoke. To me he was a legend in his own lifetime. Who knows, without Joe's excellent learn-to-play manual, snooker's undisputed Bible, I might still be a promising youngster practising hard at the Plumstead Common Working-men's Club.

2

Fees, Fights and a Fiasco

By an amazing stroke of luck – if stroke is the right word – the Surbiton branch of the St John's Ambulance Brigade landed something of a coup for their charity snooker evening at the Tolworth Sports Centre in Surrey. Several weeks before the world championships, the ambulancemen had laid down their stretchers, gazed ambitiously into the future and booked Doug Mountjoy and me for a nine-frame exhibition match to raise money for a new ambulance. To bring together the world champion and the runner-up just four days after our titanic battle at the Crucible was a touch of sheer magic.

Going to Tolworth that night was very different from my previous visit there as an amateur five years earlier. This time, a policeman stood at the door to keep back the crowds, and people formed a queue for autographs and photographs. I took the World Cup with me and the children pushed forward to the front to touch it.

Just before the match, Doug and I were approached by a commercial television company who wanted to film us during the game. Although the money they offered was attractive enough, I didn't think it fair to the BBC, the television audiences, or to myself, to build an exhibition match into something bigger than it really was. Permission was refused on these grounds, but the newspapers twisted the reasons to make it seem as though we were being mercenary, claiming that if more money had been put up, we would have given our consent. Barry and I are finding more and more that this type of sniping is becoming a common dig from people who are either jealous or want to drum up a sensational story.

I certainly wasn't bothered about the money that night, as just before the game I received £3,000 from the Atari video company for a mere fifteen-minute photographic session. My first taste of the type of money a world champion can earn!

After Tolworth, I flew out early next morning to Belfast for a four-man tournament involving Thorburn, Stevens and Higgins. Though Stevens beat me, and went on to win the event, I still achieved front-page coverage with a nice large picture of me sitting between a pair of lovely young twin girls. This annoyed Higgins. The newspaper was published somewhere near where he was born, and he was far from happy at finishing up in small print on page three.

From Belfast, I flew back to Manchester for a Sunday evening exhibition match against Cliff Thorburn. It was strange playing Cliff so soon after our behind-the-scenes bust-up at the world championships. Yet there was no animosity now. And I think it was a compliment to snooker that we could play with no lasting ill feeling and be able to enjoy a good laugh.

After the Thorburn exhibition I stayed in Manchester and enjoyed an interesting day watching Barry negotiate a twelve-month contract for me with Arthur Lamb, the Sports Editor of the *Daily Star*, to write a regular weekly column. This was fascinating, and certainly a very different world from my life on the green baize. We finally agreed a fee of £25,000, and I must admit I was pleased, though rather surprised at the amount of money.

Later on, I asked Barry to explain how he calculated the fee, to which he replied: 'Oh, it's easy. Last time our fee was £2,500, so I just added a nought!' We both laughed and agreed to try our utmost to make sure we gave first-class value. I can now say that it was the beginning of one of the best business relationships I have ever had.

Getting back to snooker, I went straight into a two-day invitation tournament at Manchester, beating Jimmy White in the final to add a further £1,000 to my piggy-bank.

Contrary to popular belief, becoming world champion did not mean an immediate whopping big pay rise. My exhibition matches had been booked up well in advance, so my nightly fee remained between £300 and £500, and in line with Ray Reardon, Cliff Thorburn and Alex Higgins at that time. After the world championships, Barry and I decided to increase my fee to £1,000 a night, but the demand was so great that we kept pushing it up, mainly in the hope that we might deter a few people so that I could get some time off.

This plan has still not worked. During the year my fee rose to £2,500, and I'm still waiting for a night off! Barry says that with a fee that size I can carry on waiting! And my dad thinks it's absolutely hilarious that I can earn more in a few days than he does in a whole year. The money is certainly nice, but I am pleased to say that it has not affected my relationships with those people who are close to me and mean something to me.

When it became common news that my fee had increased so dramatically, we received an emergency call from 'Worried' in Ogmore Vale who had booked me several months earlier for just £300. 'Worried' thought we might gazump him ... but, instead, we congratulated him on his foresight.

A typical Welsh welcome was laid on for me at the club. A bunch of friendly kids stood at the door chanting, 'Doug! Doug! Doug!' Then, as soon as I stepped inside, the secretary made a point of telling me that all the top professionals had played there, but not one of them had managed a century break. Mind you, this is a remark club stewards make all over the country. However, it was still a challenge and I responded by producing *two* centuries in the first three frames.

After the interval, seven keen members of the club all lined up, itching to dethrone me in front of their friends – and four of them did! A local reporter couldn't believe his eyes and thought he'd stumbled on the scoop of the year.

'Have you ever lost like that before?' he said. 'Is this the worst night in your life?' he rattled on.

He totally failed to see that I was only there to entertain the audience and not to win any trophies. He also conveniently forgot the two century breaks. I suppose that having made these two centuries, there was little incentive left for me. But I just couldn't get him to understand that I had achieved what I wanted and that everyone in the club was more than satisfied.

In the months that followed, I gradually became too expensive for the clubs alone to book me, and sponsors had to be found. I am delighted to recall that they have virtually bitten Barry's hands off to have me, and he's now going around looking more like Venus de Milo every day. Sponsors are always gratefully received. They have helped to raise snooker to its current high status and made a lot of top players very wealthy men.

So it was rather sad that the new Guinness tournament in the Isle of Wight should leave many players frothing at the mouth. Truth is, the promoters tried to cram a quart into a pint jar. Professionals were asked to compete in as many as three tournaments all taking place at the same time.

To make the tournament work, match times had to be altered, Eddie Charlton was dropped and reinstated, and some players, amateurs and professionals, had to start their games around midnight. One match ended as late as 2.45 in the morning. I deliberately scratched from the billiards, because it would have meant playing four consecutive matches on the same day without having a minute to eat.

Cliff Thorburn was probably the worst to suffer. After failing to appear for his 9 p.m. match against Alf Micallef, the promoters kicked him out. Though he was called three times over the loudspeakers, Thorburn never entered the arena. He was resting in his chalet half a mile away, completely unaware that he was required to play.

Once some of the professionals heard that Cliff was sacked, they put down their cues and tried to persuade Micallef to change his mind. But the Portsmouth amateur refused to budge. He said later that he had struck a blow for all amateurs who had been scratched in similar circumstances over the years. I knew what he meant, and I agreed with him.

Thorburn preferred not to comment, except to say that he didn't expect to be on the table again, having played and beaten George Campbell earlier in the day. In such chaotic conditions, I could well understand his confusion.

Led by Terry Griffiths, the professionals eventually decided against a walkout. This would have wrecked the tournament and caused any number of other serious problems as there always seems to be some type of conflict between the professional and amateur associations.

It was good to meet people there who just a few years earlier had said I would never make it as a professional. In some ways, I suppose it was very much an ego trip. Everyone, I am sure, enjoys being told he is good.

I was hooked on Space Invaders at the time, and the organisers put my favourite machine, the Defender, in a private room for me. The trouble was, the place was so small that I couldn't even take my cue from its case without bumping into the wall.

No matter where I go these days, I usually find a video-machine of some sort standing in a corner waiting for me. They turn up in dressing-rooms, hotel rooms and even club foyers. I play them whenever I can, but I must admit my enthusiasm has waned since The Defender. It seems the manufacturers reached the ultimate with this machine, and it will take something just as good to recapture my interest. Mind you, I might just have grown out of them by now!

Personally, I encountered no difficulties on or off the table during that tournament. Guinness was good for me! And it was cheers all round when I beat Mike Darrington comfortably in the Open, despite having to give him twenty-five points a frame.

Thorburn gained some consolation for his earlier disappointments when he and fellow-Canadian Natalie Stelmach beat John Virgo and Vera Selby in the mixed pairs final after John and Vera had eliminated Ann Johnson and me in the semi-finals.

Vera was in fine form. Earlier in the week, she had won the women's world championships as well. Though she does not have the flair of some other women players, she certainly beats them all on tactics. This is a crucial part of their game because, until women's snooker reaches a higher standard, the tactician will usually come out on top.

Women's snooker is bound to improve over the next few years and it is something I would really welcome, as it can only further improve the image of the game. A lot of women players are consistently making breaks of forty and fifty, but not one is capable of mustering a hundred in any regular fashion.

I believe women are not as good as men because they don't possess the same ability to concentrate over long periods. Snooker is not a physical game, so muscular strength and stamina cannot be used to explain the enormous gap that exists between the sexes. Having said that, I am still convinced that once they learn to apply themselves mentally over extended spells and perhaps develop something of a killer instinct, women are going to improve in leaps and bounds in snooker circles. Of course, it would be fantastic for the game if a woman player could break through as a professional, although I am not too sure whether I would want to be beaten by one!

Straight after the Guinness tournament, Cliff and I were booked for a three-frame novelty game in a television studio in Edinburgh to go out live as a prelude to the Scottish Cup Final. By the time the final against Darrington had finished all the ferries had stopped for the night, so a helicopter was brought in to fly me to Gatwick to connect with a Scottish flight. It was my first trip in a helicopter and I certainly enjoyed it.

My match with Cliff finished early, so we were both invited to join the panel of soccer experts to comment on the Scottish Cup Final. All my years as a loyal Charlton Athletic supporter were about to pay off, at last!

The English Cup Final was played on the same day and I had the rare privilege of watching both matches on monitor sets in the studio. With my head swinging to and fro, it was a bit like Wimbledon. I made lots of notes in order to give my opinion, but just when my turn arrived, the producer waved his arms frantically and told us we had run out of time.

Prestatyn was my next port of call. It's about the farthest you can go in North Wales without getting wet. It's also the home of the annual Pontin's Festival, a one-week snooker jamboree that brings together the best of our amateurs and professionals.

For once, I was unable to concentrate. I wasn't with it. Terry Griffiths beat me in the first round of the professional tournament and John Hargreaves put me out of the pro-am section.

Without being derogatory about either man, I had subconsciously decided to stop playing snooker for a week and I was quickly punished. Both players maintained their form through the week and went on to win their respective tournaments.

With Pontin's over, I took a rare chance to relax at a boxing match. Along with Barry, I was invited as guest of honour by the Manchester Sporting Club to attend my first live boxing evening. Lots of people came up asking for my autograph and also kept asking Barry, thinking he was a snooker player. Barry signed so many pieces of paper that by the end of the night, I think he really believed he was a snooker star, although the whole of Romford knows differently!

In fairness to Barry, he is shrewd enough when playing for money.

He has a unique knack of picking out opponents who usually stand little chance of beating him.

On one visit to Plymouth, he played Herman Bond, a local farmer, and owner of the St Mellion Golf and Country Club. As Barry loves a bet, he didn't need any pushing when his wife Susan jokingly said she fancied a lamb. He immediately said he would play Herman at snooker, putting up thirty pounds to a lamb for every frame.

At one stage, Barry was almost a flock in front, and was talking of going through Yellow Pages to find Rent-a-Wagon to carry the lambs back to Essex.

'I'm going to be a shepherd!' he kept repeating. 'I won't have to mow the lawn any more. . . .'

Unfortunately, as the night drew on, Herman the farmer dug his plough in, and Barry ended up being milked!

The Manchester boxers put on a fine display, and I turned to Barry and admitted that this was the first time I had really appreciated how easily I earn my money compared with some other people. The worst that can happen to me when I lose is to walk from the arena with my head hanging low. Some boxers are lucky to leave with their head still attached. That's not all. When I win, I usually stick my teeth into a rare steak. When a boxer wins, he is more likely to stick it over his eye. Though I enjoy watching boxers battling it out, I don't watch the sport as a purist. I merely like it for its aggression and for the atmosphere and noise it generates.

Personally, I am not the boxing type. When did you last see a guy fight for a world championship in evening dress? No, I'm an out-and-out physical coward. I am still the only chap to have his cash refunded from Charles Atlas!

Looking closely at snooker and boxing, I believe there is a real similarity between the demands made on the participants. Boxers, like snooker players, are in the arena alone. Both need courage, tenacity and the psychological power to hit back when the going gets rough. The mental pressures are very much the same. And ultimately, of course, the men involved stand or fall by their own performance. There is no team-mate to dig them out. Both are involved in head-to-head confrontations, only it's the boxer who comes away with the visible scars. Ours are only mental, but real, all the same.

In some ways, I suppose, a boxer might be better off. At least he is always in a position to defend himself. This is not always the case in snooker, where a player can be left sitting helplessly in his corner while his opponent dominates the game at the table, leaving him no opportunity to hit back.

I'm afraid I dropped my guard a little one night when attending the National Sporting Club in London for Ken Buchanan's last fight, and ended up taking a self-inflicted psychological blow on the chin.

The night's Master of Ceremonies invited me to join Henry Cooper in the ring to draw some lucky numbers from a box. As I stepped through the ropes, I feinted to throw a right hand at Henry, and suddenly realised the mistake and tried to check myself, but I was too late. I noticed the look on Henry's face as I went to sling the punch, and I regretted it for the rest of the night. The move was as original as someone saying to me, 'I'll give you two blacks' start, Steve!'

3

A Boob on Page Three

In June, Barry and I made a colossal mistake in allowing a newspaper reporter to travel, and virtually live, with me for a whole week. It was nothing more than a snooping exercise. A Davisgate!

The reporter wanted to know if I ironed my shirts, washed my socks, what I ate for breakfast, how I generally coped living from a suitcase, and just about every other personal detail you could imagine.

Though the newspaper paid for the privilege, we realised we had made a terrible blunder in granting them such an intrusion, and we are sure nothing of that nature will happen again. When someone like that is constantly in the car with you, walks the streets with you, eats alongside you, and is making notes on everything you do, it is impossible to conduct any sort of private life.

I probably value my privacy more than most people, because I am hounded, day in, day out, by one reporter or another. I am not complaining about straight interviewing because, if nothing else, it confirms that someone, somewhere, still believes I'm worth including in their news columns. The time to worry is when people stop wanting to know about me.

Driving three-hundred miles a day may be a terrible slog, but it does, at least, provide one guaranteed way of being on my own, and

I can pull up for petrol and have a pee without anyone taking out a pencil and making a note of it. That, I suppose, is the length and breadth of my privacy these days.

On the reporter's third day with me, I played Alex Higgins in an exhibition match in Margate. Of course, it is well known that matches between Higgins and me are no ordinary, tame games of snooker. They are more like a fireworks display.

Winning means everything to both of us. And I am sure that it is this burning desire to be superior at all times that causes so much of the fuss and friction between us. We both need to feed our egos, and it's noticeable that when we do confront each other, our will to win intensifies.

Margate was no exception. We set out to play the best of nine frames in front of a packed hall. The crowd was buzzing, and by the time the night was over, no one left there disappointed.

The dramatic high-spot came when Higgins, leading by four frames to three, potted the blue and cringed as he saw the white ball shoot across the table and fly in-off. In such a case, the rules state clearly that I should be given five points and Alex nothing. But not this time. The scoreboard, manned by two Ladbrokes girls, correctly added five points to my total, but also incorrectly gave five points to Alex for potting the blue.

At first, I didn't notice the mistake, and worked out instead that I needed a snooker to save the frame. It was only after playing my shot that I realised the score was wrong and protested to the referee. As you would expect, Alex also protested, but I genuinely believe he had no idea how the mess-up occurred.

Of course, the referee was powerless. The scores could not be altered. So Alex went away winning by five frames to three. On this occasion it was the referee's mistake, but as the Ladbrokes girls were in charge of the score, *I'll betcha* they don't do the job again! Seriously, though, none of this would have happened if the organisers had appointed an official scorer to record the points in the way they do at nearly all our tournaments.

In fact, Alex himself suffered in the Scottish Masters in Glasgow when a referee short-changed him during a break and no scorer was at hand to correct the error.

From time to time I like to get well away from tournaments and exhibition matches. I like to come out of my shell and let myself go.

I might even get paralytic now and again! But I always do it when there are no matches to worry about, and when no one is around to report on it. Surely everyone is entitled to a good night out once in a while?

Early in the summer, Barry decided to put on a celebration party at Romford for Vic Harris and me. It was a tribute to Vic for winning the English amateur and for me winning the world championships.

The party was for all the local regulars, plus a number of invited guests. And just to prove it was a party, Vic and I walked to the match table weighed down with champagne and glasses. Just below us, Barry had transformed his office into a disco-cum-buffet parlour with the jukebox clanging, food for a month, and enough lager to keep Bill Werbeniuk afloat.

Still not satisfied, Barry laid on a cabaret of three comedians just to be sure we didn't go short of laughs. Mike Reid, Charlie Smithers and Tony Dowling topped the bill in a fantastic funny night. But even then, with the jokes flowing, I still nipped in and stole the show with the most remarkable shot I have ever played.

The white ball was placed directly behind the blue in the centre of the table and straight in line with the bottom right-hand pocket. I was left with a simple, straightforward shot, and I was getting down to play it when Mike Reid piped up and said, 'Okay, son, I could get that with my eyes shut.'

To which I replied: 'So where would you like it?'

He smiled, thought for a while, and said: 'Up here, mate, in this hole' – and pointed to the pocket just under his arm, behind me, in the bottom right-hand corner. The audience coughed and spluttered and saw it as the best gag of the night.

To achieve the pot, the blue needed to be played at precise angles off four cushions and with the enormous power. I was drunk!

I slammed the blue, watched it strike the three top cushions, shoot across to the far-side cushion and finally rocket back into the bottom right-hand corner pocket where I was standing, without touching the sides.

I couldn't believe it. No one could believe it. The whole of Romford stood up and cheered. I turned round and found that Mike Reid had dropped to the floor in disbelief. Eventually, he got to his feet and congratulated me. Apart from that, he was lost for words, which was more remarkable than the shot itself!

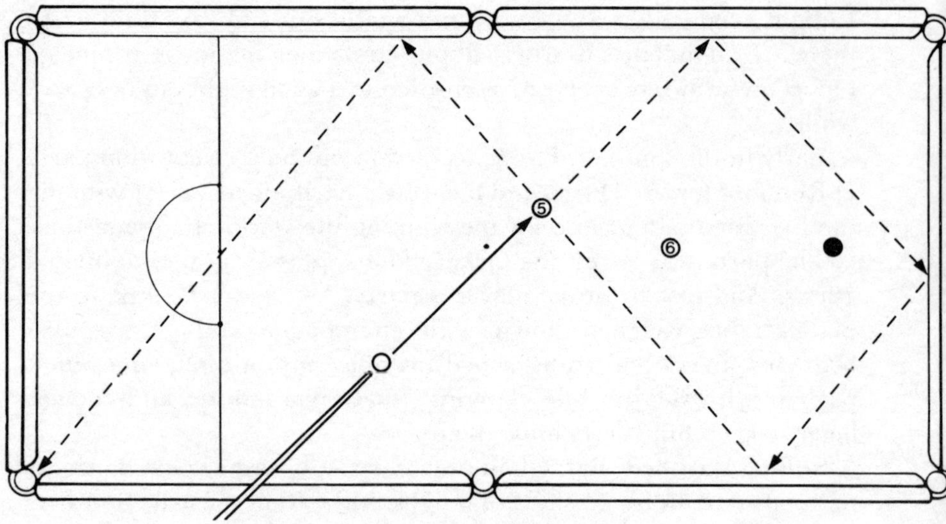

My party piece: potting the blue off four cushions.

Halfway through the party, I noticed a man drinking alongside the jukebox. He didn't leave his seat all night. Meanwhile a woman kept ringing up asking if her husband was with us, and Barry went on saying that he wasn't there. In the end, she rang up to say that she had reported him missing to the police. Several hours later we realised that the man she wanted was the one sitting near the jukebox. He was one of Barry's hall assistants, but Barry was too cross-eyed to notice.

He finally left about three in the morning to walk home. Around halfway, his legs were so weak that he stopped and noticed two horses in a field behind a hedge. One of them was quite big, and the other no higher than a child's pony. So he went into the field and tried to climb on the back of the big horse, but it was too tall for him. Determined not to give up, he turned to the pony and this time successfully scrambled on to its back.

With his legs dangling down the sides, he set off like John Wayne to ride into town, but the posse was waiting for him in the shape of flashing blue lights, and he was taken in by the sheriff and given a complimentary room for the night. It was that type of party!

Dave Muscroft, an excellent snooker photographer, also suffered a few getting-home pains. He, too, turned down a taxi and decided to walk five miles to his hotel. Barry found him at six in the morning, flat out on a roundabout, his camera over a shoulder and a bottle of spirits in each pocket. His white tuxedo made it look as though he'd just come off Tiswas!

For a change, I moved into a different type of frame a day or two later, sitting for portrait artist Peter Deighan at his studio in Luton. Who said I'm no oil painting?

Before I arrived, I thought I'd have to remain absolutely still, like a lump of porcelain, for hours on end, but it was not a bit like that. I was allowed to move about in my chair, chat freely, and drink tea by the gallon. Though I must admit I found it a little strange having someone looking so close at every – well, almost every – part of my body.

Eventually, Barry and I decided to produce a limited edition of 250 prints to give them some exclusive value. The canvas measures twenty-four inches by eighteen, and is enclosed in a heavy gold frame. Each portrait is also individually signed and stamped.

Talking of pictures, I always cringe when I see a girl heading my way with a scrapbook to sign, because it invariably contains the topless picture of me that appeared on the front page of the *Daily Star* on the day after I won the world championships.

I shall never forget posing for that picture. The photographer said, 'Okay, I'm ready now. Tense your muscles.'

Gritting my teeth, I replied: 'I already am!'

With the summer almost upon us, the snooker season was practically over. Barry and I had been invited to a number of golf tournaments and we practised like rookies. For someone like me, forever cooped up in airless halls, golf offers a wonderful way to relax. I am not madly in love with the game, and I have no ambition to take it up seriously, but I do appreciate the many skills involved.

I regard golf as an escape route. Like Space Invaders. An opportunity to get out of the pressure-cooker and be able to perform in public without scrutiny from large crowds and television cameras – although that was far from the case when I played in the Coral Pro-Am at Royal Porthcawl.

Barry, Del Simmons and I formed a team to represent snooker, expertly assisted by Sandy Lyle, one of Britain's leading professionals.

Right from the start I couldn't stop shaking. Barry was worse. Once he realised he had to hit the ball in front of a crowd and those television cameras, he rushed off to the bar for a stiffener. Only his nerves were so bad that when he picked up his Bacardi and Coke the glass slipped through his quivering fingers and crashed to the floor. The thought of missing the ball in front of all those people was too much for him. His bottle had gone in more ways than one!

All too soon, like waiting at the dentist's, it was our turn to suffer. An announcer called out each player's name one by one. . . . 'And on the tee now, Steve Davis, world snooker champion.' I felt my whole body shake like a jelly.

Considering my state of nerves, I was amazed I actually hit the ball. At first, I even thought it was a good shot, but then discovered that the ball had decided to veer off course and bury itself in the worst of the Porthcawl rough. Time and again Barry and I drove out of bounds while Del Simmons, an accomplished golfer, and Sandy Lyle were regularly hitting straight down the middle.

A large crowd followed us off the first tee, but by the time we reached the third, they were down to single figures. As we trooped off the third, I overheard Sandy saying to Del, 'It looks as though we're on our own!' How right he was. Our team was doomed from the start.

Despite the frustrations, the round itself proved a great laugh. When it became clear that we couldn't win any type of prize, Barry started betting on individual holes with David Brimacombe of Corals.

They tried every trick imaginable, and pulled more strokes than the Oxford boat crew.

Robbo, the Billy Connolly of Romford, kept asking Barry if he should drop a few spare balls around the greens to make it easy for him, but when Barry finally said yes, he found there was not one left in the bag. Barry had lost them all in the rough.

Close to one hole, with Barry well placed to win a bet at last, David 'accidentally' ran over his ball in the Coral buggy, and then 'accidentally' reversed over it, pressing it into the ground and leaving it virtually impossible to strike. Refused a free drop, Barry continued to go farther and farther behind in the betting stakes.

By the eighteenth he stood to lose a fortune. So he doubled the lot and attempted to get past Sandy's drive in two shots. His first flew out of bounds, so he again doubled up, and his next bounced into the rough.

The bet continued to be doubled and, after about a dozen shots, Barry finally came within a hundred yards of the green, but with his ball precariously placed on the edge of a bunker. In a state of panic, he again doubled the bet, this time against getting down in four from this hopeless position.

For his final surge to the green, Barry decided to use a sand-wedge. And the ball moved two inches! In a real frenzy, he took a wild hack and sent the ball flying to the front of the green, but still well short of the flag.

He now had just two shots left to win his bet. And if you know the eighteenth at Porthcawl you will appreciate his predicament. It is more like a marines' training ground than a golf course, with dips and hollows everywhere. By now I was very much a spectator, having run out of balls and given up. I settled on admiring the aesthetic beauty of the lovely Porthcawl coastline.

The bet was still on, and Barry had two shots left to save his shirt. He was all of forty feet from the hole and frantic at the thought of losing his money. So instead of asking for Robbo's advice, he decided to chat up Sandy Lyle's caddie, the one and only Jimmy Dickinson. Anything not to pay Brimacombe.

Whispering softly, Jimmy told Barry to aim his ball at an imaginary hole three feet away from the ball, slightly to the right and up the bank.

'But it will never reach!' croaked Barry. But Jimmy insisted: 'Do as I say and you may just hold on to your money.'

Money? The word almost caused a convulsion. Barry did just as he was told and he watched the ball zig-zag like a snake and amazingly end up just six inches from the hole.

Happy now, Barry walked up, tapped the ball in and, with a huge smile, raised his fist to tumultuous cheers from the crowd, who clearly thought he had birdied the hole. Of course, they hadn't seen him earlier, struggle like Percy Thrower in the undergrowth.

Sandy Lyle then came along and gracefully rolled in a difficult six-footer for a real birdie three, but the crowd responded with a mere ripple, clearly baffled as to why Sandy was keeping Barry out of the Ryder Cup team.

4

Fame at Last

Television, of course, continues to play a considerable part in my life. After the laughs of Porthcawl, I was next to face the cameras in a new BBC series called *Fame*.

At first they filmed me discussing my weekly column at the *Daily Star* offices with Sports Editor Arthur Lamb, who immediately became an overnight star, managing to mention his paper's name at least twelve times.

The crew were a great laugh, headed by producer Nick Handle, and presenter John (don't mention *Braden's Week*) Pitman.

The battalion later moved on to Arthur Barker, the publishers of my autobiography, and I was interviewed with their managing director, Stephen du Sautoy, with Barry inevitably providing the inter-round summaries. Some people have said that every time Barry opened his mouth, the word money came jingling out. Still, perhaps that's what being a good manager is all about!

The crew were keen to take some off-beat film of me out in the air relaxing, and Corals came to the rescue by inviting me to present the prizes at their sponsored Eclipse Stakes meeting at Sandown.

When the *Daily Star* heard I would be at the racecourse, they asked me to select a horse for each of the six races, and to include them in my column on the morning of the meeting. I know as much about racing as Barry knows about cue-action, so I borrowed a bent pin, sorted out six, and the best I could manage was one short-priced winner and three that finished second. So I'm not retiring yet!

As a kid, I remember watching horse-racing on television with my mother and thinking that Lester Piggott won every race, and that there was nothing difficult in picking winners. In the Coral race, I went for a horse called Hard Fought. And I had a bet with the bookmakers, just to put my money where my mouth was.

Having laid out the cash, I fancied a look at my nag, and when I saw him in the paddock I really believed he was raring to go. What I didn't know, and found out some thirty seconds later, was that he was walking round behind an attractive filly called Vielle, and what was going through his fertile mind was clear to everyone.

'Look,' I said to Barry, 'I've picked a horse with five legs!'

Hard Fought had less interest in the race than I had. The dirty devil was only there for Vielle! He must have shed half a stone before he reached the starting-post. Needless to say, he didn't win, spending half the race with his eye on Vielle. As it turned out, he was beaten by Master Willie, and if that's not ironic, then I don't know what is!

Shortly afterwards, I flew direct from Heathrow to Miami to board the Nordic Prince for a fortnight's sleep-and-sunshine cruise to the Caribbean. Before leaving, I had to put the finishing touches to my autobiography, and I reached the airport with just fifteen minutes left before take-off. This was my first holiday for five years, and with the way my diary was filling up with exhibition matches, tournaments, promotional work and foreign tours, I realised it could be the last for another ten.

Even then, Barry was reluctant to give me a complete break. He checked that I was carrying a pen and reminded me that I had less than a month to complete a book on how to play snooker for the Letts company, to be published under their World of Sport banner.

So instead of tripping round the ballroom every night, I was up on deck, struggling to put my thoughts on paper. The book sets out to advise the young and not-so-young on how best to learn the game of snooker. And to make it simple for readers of all ages to go off and practice, a large number of diagrams are used to back up my words.

I had looked forward to the challenge of writing such a book, and it brought back clear memories of the endless hours my father and I spent using Joe Davis's marvellous instructional manual to correct my early faults.

Now, I was in a position to produce a similar book, and this gave me a good feeling. It made me proud that young people were going to listen to my advice, and it was good for my father, too. During those early years, we studied the game hard and learnt a lot from just trial and error. But we've come a long way since, and I'm obviously delighted I was so keen and devoted to learning, and that my father had so much patience and was always at hand to encourage me.

I'm sure the book will give a lot of help to many people, but no one should run off with the idea that he or she can learn all about snooker in only a year. If they do, then many parents are going to be disappointed. Learning about snooker is a hard, long slog. There are no short cuts, no magic formulas. It's all about practice and dedication. If you've got flair and talent, then work on them. Like a good garden, your game won't blossom without attention.

During my formative years, I took a lot of stick for being too mechanical. I didn't let it bother me. My father insisted that I developed an impeccable basic technique. And it's on this firm foundation that the rest of my play has been built.

These days I fear no one. A combination of technique and consistency appears to have put me comfortably in front of any other player in the game. Of course, I shall lose a tournament or two from time to time, but then I'm only human after all. Honestly!

I think television has now proved beyond doubt that everyone has to work hard to keep up with me. I know there is no one around who can concentrate long enough to be a serious threat to my dominating most major tournaments. If all matches could be played over one hundred frames, then I'd be a certainty every time. But whether my dad could stand the tension, is another matter.

I came back from the Caribbean literally in the pink. Not exactly my favourite colour, but definitely the next best. I was fresh and ready for business.

Barry noticed that, too. Before I had time to unpack properly, he was whisking me off to the West Country to discuss a lucrative promotional offer from Leisure Industries, a young company who produce a wide range of snooker tables under the brand name of Pot Black. At first they thought of producing just a Steve Davis deluxe model, but after several hours of talking we all decided that I should

Just where I like to be – in the driving seat!

This takes Courage!

Mike Reid entertains the crowd at the Romford celebration . . . and is about to challenge me to my hardest shot ever – a pot off four cushions.

'You must be joking! – but I'll try!'

Total chaos. Even Charlie Smithers can't believe it's in. . . .

Trying to trap the Silver Fox during the Jameson Open.

'I've enjoyed watching some great snooker,' jokes Dennis Taylor after his 9–0 whitewash.

Getting down to basics with my dad, my sternest critic and staunchest supporter.

Going to the dogs . . . presenting the Lucania Gold Cup at the Coral track in Romford.

Definitely not favourite this time. Snooker professionals go golfing at Wentworth.

We are the champions – though you wouldn't think it! England win State Express world team championships.

Tony's got it taped. Visiting comedian Tony Dowling's video shop in Sheffield.

Tony Meo celebrates joining us at the Romford stable.

put my name to their entire range, which extends right through all sizes from two feet to six feet.

My contract with Leisure Industries lasts three years with further options afterwards. In all, it should earn me around £500,000 and is by far the largest agreement I have signed up to now for endorsing a product. Like most people, my first game of snooker was played on a small table, and it's encouraging to see that the quality of these tables is improving all the time.

I must put on record that I have enjoyed working with the Pot Black team who are very keen and extremely professional. Overall, I believe that being a young company and growing together has provided the biggest incentive. They went public in 1982, and I was happy to buy a chunk of shares along with Barry. Pot Black are part of the Steve Davis camp, and hardly a week goes by without some involvement between us. And that's the way I like it.

Still dreaming of my nights in the Caribbean, I went straight up to Leicester, hardly exotic when set alongside Barbados, and with my head drifting off to sandy shores, I was inevitably washed aside by Jimmy White in a nine-frame exhibition match.

Neither of us realised it at the time, but this was to be the first of many fierce, tight and controversial clashes during the months ahead.

Because I had spent five days in the West Indies, an optimistic Barry evidently thought I had picked up some useful tips on how to bat, so he selected me for his Celebrity Eleven to play his club side, The Victorians.

Barry won the toss and put The Victorians in. 'Shrewd move,' he kept repeating, even when The Victorians had amassed 226 runs for just three wickets in forty overs. From the way he kept talking, I truly did believe that he thought I could do on the cricket field what I do on the snooker table.

'Steve, I'm promoting you from number ten to number five,' he said, no doubt also remembering my previous outing with The Victorians when I finished top scorer with eleven.

Alas, the memories were soon shattered by a real blinder from Dave, the hairy monster, who smashed my stumps after just three balls. Yet, even with 'Boycott' gone, all was far from lost. Helped by a few ringers from one or two counties, and with Barry leading us like Ben Hur, the Celebrity Eleven fought back and eventually strolled home by five wickets and with six overs to spare.

Though I enjoy cricket, it has never topped my list. The ball's too hard! On one occasion, while playing for The Victorians, I was asked to field near the bat at short square point. The other side had a huge Pakistani who loved to slog. He hit Barry for three consecutive fours, and our captain decided to replace him with a slow off-spin bowler who just lobbed the ball up.

Whenever I play in the team, Barry spends most of his time taking care to keep me away from the firing line in case I damage my hands, but this time something went drastically wrong. The third ball was a gentle teaser near the off-stump and the Pakistani threw his whole body behind it. The bat connected with the ball and it flew like a red-hot meteorite into the pit of my stomach. It was there before I knew it had left the bat.

My hands dropped instinctively to the point of the pain. I was doubled up, with the ball stuck in my pouch. I rolled over and over and finally held the ball up in one hand. As soon as the other players saw it, they dashed over and congratulated me, convinced that I had taken the catch of the season.

In my first game for Barry's team, he even asked me to bowl. The first ball was so bad that the batsman at the non-striker's end said he would give his wicket away just to get my autograph. From the next ball, the batsman scored a run, and the big-shot non-striker had his chance to deal with me. I pitched the ball just outside his off-stump and in trying to thump me into Romford High Street, he got a nick and was caught by the wicket-keeper. He tried to say he did it deliberately to get my autograph, so I signed his bat for his kids.

With my twenty-fourth birthday, on 22 August approaching fast, Barry insisted that I spent a few days at home with him and Susan and their two young children, Katie and Edward. Barry said he wanted me to work a little more on my *Successful Snooker* book.

At this stage, there was absolutely no hint of his real motive for luring me to Ongar. And it wasn't until the third day, the night before my birthday, that I realised we had done nothing on the book and sensed that something strange was going on.

For some weeks I had nagged him that my Rover was a cripple and had to be put down. We discussed buying a Porsche, but Barry maintained there were serious delivery problems and that one wouldn't be available until after Christmas.

To be sure I didn't sleep late on my birthday, Barry arranged an early-morning call which involved sending Edward in to punch me on the nose. I recommend it strongly as the best way of waking up instantly. After Edward had raised the alarm, Katie rushed in with a jar of after-shave as a gift, and Edward handed me a small leather case with 'Porsche' written on the outside.

I thought, 'This will be great when I get my car,' and put it down at the bedside.

Barry then stuck his head round the door and said, 'I see you've not looked inside it yet. . . .' To which I chuckled and said, 'Oh, God, don't say you've got the car!'

The key was inside, all right. A massive key. Large enough to unlock Wormwood Scrubs. I pulled on a pair of pants, dashed to the big window that overlooks the drive, and there, down below, was this gleaming white Porsche. It had been in Barry's garage for three days. I was lost for words.

5

In for the Kill

With September approaching, the snooker season was starting to warm up. By now my cheap-rate engagements had almost ended and I was ready to charge the type of fee you would expect from the world champion. Barry kept repeating, 'If you want a Ferrari, then you don't pay Ford prices.'

Having still not fully shaken off my holiday mood, I wasn't cueing all that well when the season's first major tournament came along. Yet it was a nice big carrot, and I was determined to do well. Jameson Whiskey, entirely new sponsors in snooker, had come forward with more than £66,000 in hard cash, including £20,000 for the winner, and a further £100,000 if anyone could achieve the maximum break.

This appealed to me. After all, by tradition September is a sleepy month for doing little more than a few exhibition matches and starting to loosen the cue action again.

The Jameson is a genuine Open event with invitations extended to every professional in the world. I had barely a week to prepare for it after my holidays, and I split the time between playing in exhibition matches and driving up and down the motorway. Barry booked me for a string of engagements as far apart as Burnley, Eltham, Peterborough, Croydon and Edinburgh. He reckoned it paid better than mowing the lawn.

The schedule was so tight that I arrived up to ninety minutes late for my Edinburgh exhibition against Higgins. Of course, that is one of the constant hazards of the job, calculating distances and allowing for traffic jams, particularly for matches played in the afternoons. I took some stick for not being on time, but I can truthfully say that it's the only exhibition match for which I've kept people waiting and, with my work-rate, I think it's a record I can be proud of.

I already knew that my first Jameson opponent would be the winner of the qualifying match between Perrie Mans and Tony Meo. Tiny Tony, the Spaghetti Kid, had just parted with his long-time manager Henry West and joined me and Vic Harris at Romford under Barry's expert control.

At first Barry was reluctant to take Tony on, mainly because he thought it might affect the great relationship that had built up between him and me. We discussed the matter a lot, but I knew that feelings ran so deeply between us that nothing like this could spoil it in any way.

My only doubts hinged on how I would feel when I played Tony in a match. Then I sat down and thought about it, and I was satisfied that the new arrangements would have no effect on me, so he was welcomed into the fold.

Tony is a great guy and deserves the best. I enjoy playing against good sportsmen, and Tony is definitely one of them. Barry told Tony he would do everything for him, but also warned him, 'Whenever you are playing Steve, you know whose side I'll be on.' Tony accepted that like a man. He was obviously delighted to be involved with a happy team, and with a successful, well organised manager.

The squad grew even bigger a few months later when Terry Griffiths joined us. Barry had just sold his chain of Lucania snooker halls to Riley Leisure, and this meant he had a bit more time available to manage players. Of course, Terry is a model professional and Barry was clearly delighted that he should agree to join our team at Romford. Barry again asked for my views first, but I still had no objections because I knew it could not affect our relationship.

With Terry signed up, one or two wise-guys asked Barry if he would now be taking a course in Welsh to understand what he said. Barry said no – but he would be sending Terry to Romford Polytechnic to learn to speak proper!

Back at the Jameson, it seemed as though I would be playing Tony in my first game of the new season, and would know straight away whether we had made the right decision. But Perrie Mans, probably the most unpredictable of all the top players, again upset the form-book by knocking him out in the qualifying rounds.

Mans had beaten me in the Benson and Hedges Masters earlier in the year, depriving me of the only major title in what could have been a memorable Grand Slam, so I was determined to gain revenge and was in no mood to let him repeat the defeat.

Cueing well, I slipped into a comfortable 2–0 lead, but once more Perrie's amazing unorthodoxy brought him back into the game. He levelled at 3–3 and there were real signs that Mr Jinx was going to cast his spell over me again.

During the interval, while leading 3–1, I left the arena to freshen up, and it was so dark behind the curtains that I walked straight into a wooden partition and banged my right shoulder. The crash was so loud it echoed through the hall and everyone gasped, convinced the roof was caving in. When I returned to the table, I lost the next two frames, and the Press were quickly knocking out stories like: Has he ripped the muscles in his arm? Did the bump affect his game? Is he really made of steel, and didn't feel a thing?

Frankly, the bump never crossed my mind. The arm stayed in one piece, the cue action remained as reliable as ever, and after Perrie's brief surge, I was not extended to win the next two frames to qualify to meet David Taylor in the quarter-final.

As always, the Silver Fox was licking his lips at the prospect of a big kill and immediately ran off with the first frame. I was soon on his trail, however, grabbed hold of him and wouldn't put him down. I killed him off 5–1 with a series of solid breaks to reach the seventeen-frame semi-final where I was to play the belligerent Alex Higgins, a confrontation I approached with very much the same attitude as a lion-tamer entering the cage to control and discipline a pacing cat.

Before I could even consider the Higgins game, I had to squeeze in a flight to Jersey for an exhibition match which Barry had arranged for me several months earlier. I flew there in a six-seater light aircraft, along with Kirk Stevens and Tony Meo. To be sure of making the flight, I was out of bed at six and drove to Castle Donington to board at eight o'clock. This was my first experience of going up in a light aircraft, and I found it totally different from all those luxury trips I had enjoyed in jumbo jets. It was no flight for cowards. The strong wind tossed us around like a shuttlecock. We dipped sharply several times and my stomach shook hands with my throat. I wasn't bored a bit!

Flying generally excites me a lot. I never think of crashes or bad landings. If I'm flying across the world, I usually drop my seat back, close my eyes and fall asleep. I always end up more scared when I come home from air trips – once I get back in my car and set off on the motorway.

I played all day in Jersey, flew back to Castle Donington next morning, again waking at six, and drove on to Derby to face Higgins in what became one of the most thrilling matches I can remember.

As I was due on the table at two o'clock, there was just enough time for an hour's shut-eye before picking up my cue and going into battle. Not surprisingly, I arrived in the arena walking on my knees, but still managed to win the all-important first frame. In normal circumstances I would have been disappointed to reach the interval with a 4–4 score against Higgins, but on this occasion I was delighted to have done so well, considering the tired state I was in.

It continued to be a riveting, see-saw game with never more than one frame separating us. Then Higgins suddenly threatened to break loose in frame fourteen when he took advantage of a stupid mistake. With the frame wrapped up, I saw no point in staggering on and I conceded on the yellow. Higgins then produced an excellent break of ninety-five and I found myself one frame adrift again, with just two to play. All good, gripping stuff, and the crowd loved it.

I broke badly in frame sixteen, leaving Higgins a simple red, but in potting the red, Higgins attempted a cannon on the black and knocked that ball in as well. This was just the let-off I needed. I jumped at the chance, ran up a quick break of forty-six, and then went back to the table for a further thirty-four to win the frame convincingly and give myself the vital psychological advantage as we came up for the last frame.

Even then the alarm-bells were ringing, and I knew that one mistake could be enough to see the new tournament slip out of sight. I galvanised myself, put my head down and assembled a quality break of ninety-five with some really satisfying snooker, and never allowed Higgins even a look at the table.

To finish a match with a big break without letting my opponent leave his seat makes me feel good and is very reassuring. If you're going to win a fight, then knock him out!

Weary and flagging, I was glad to see the semi-final go out of sight. At last I could have a night's sleep – for the first time in a week. Even then I struggled to keep my eyes open long enough to watch the final frame played back on the video.

My parents have spent a fortune collecting tapes of me in action and when I have time to watch them, I do it solely to relive old glories and not with a view to improving my play. Unlike cricket or golf, where studying video recordings might help a player iron out certain technical flaws, snooker is more of a situation game, in which the balls are rarely, if ever, in the same place twice. Bad shots can't be corrected simply by deciding to play them differently next time because that so-called next time hardly ever comes around. The only technical benefit I derive is seeing whether I am playing my shots too fast. Whether I am missing potable balls through speeding up.

In truth, I enjoy watching myself on the video machine. The matches remind me a lot of those James Bond films. Loads of drama, impossible escapes, and with me usually ending up the hero. I suppose that's what I enjoy most about them. It is also a good opportunity to compare my performances with those of the other players. It is encouraging to see that my cue action is so much better than theirs. I look more in control of the situation.

As a bonus in the Jameson, the sponsors put up a crate of whiskey for the highest break scored every day. Up till the semi-finals I had failed to get into the spirit of things, but then Alex and I made breaks of 95 and we each received a crate to take away.

Dennis Taylor had smashed dark horse Dave Martin 9–1 in the other semi, so the crowd were all keyed up and expecting a long and competitive final. I had different ideas. I set my mind on making it a swift, clinical and convincing performance. Dennis is about the nicest fellow in the game, but I was in no mood to be generous with him.

I launched my attack feeling fresh and urgent. I was cueing perfectly. I was at my peak – relaxed, positive, and seeing the pockets as big as buckets. I raced to a 4–0 lead, and in a marvellous fifth frame I carefully put together a break of 135, the highest of the tournament, to earn myself a further £2,000. I was flying at this point, and another century break followed in frame six when I finished off with a classic 105 clearance. Keeping up the onslaught, I then collected the next two frames as well, to reach the interval with an overwhelming 8–0 lead.

When we returned for the evening session, the arena was crammed tight with people who had come in for the kill. They were not to be disappointed. Feeling in great form, I quickly took the ninth and final frame to pick up the handsome £20,000 prize, leaving Dennis to pocket £10,000 as a bemused, yet very sporting, runner-up.

There was no better way to begin my year as the world champion. It was an instant and emphatic reply to those cynics who might have thought – and even hoped – that I wouldn't cope with the pressure of proving that I was a worthy and legitimate holder of the title. My supporters' club had nothing to fear. I knew I was the best, and I knew I would get better.

Shortly after receiving my cheque, Barry told me that Higgins had walked into the hall earlier in the day, demanding his £2,000 as the player with the highest break. He couldn't wait for the tournament to finish. Much earlier in the tournament, Higgins had knocked in a sparkling 116. The promoter, however, stood firm and told him that a match was still in progress, and that he must wait until it was over before he could be paid. To which Alex replied, 'There is no way anyone is going to beat my 116.'

The words had barely left his lips when someone rushed up to him and announced that I had just scored a 135. Alex apparently threw his arms in the air and yelled, 'Hell, I've only been here two minutes and I've lost two thousand already!'

Since then, many knowledgeable people have assured me that my 9–0 win was the very first whitewash in the final of a major snooker tournament. Dennis played much better than the score indicates, and there were one or two frames early on which could easily have gone his way. He began the frames confidently enough, but as they moved on, he let them slip away and lost authority. This is a common failing among players. And it's even more pronounced and noticeable when they are playing in awe of their opponent.

Dennis is such an excellent sportsman that, when asked in an interview for his comments on the match, he replied, 'Well, to tell the truth, I've spent the whole day watching some great snooker!'

Television commentator Rex Williams, an experienced professional himself, paid me a nice compliment when he said on the air, 'I never thought anyone could dominate the modern game like this when so many tournaments are played. Steve is miles ahead of everyone.'

6

Stung into Action

Again there was no respite for me. No chance to bask in glory, even if I wanted to. With the £22,000 Jameson cheque in my pocket, I drove north to Glasgow to bid for the £22,000 Langs Supreme Masters title at the vast Kelvin Hall, a haven for many boxing champions over the years.

After my demolition job on Dennis, the Press headlined me as a good thing for a quick follow-up success.

I began impressively enough, trouncing Doug Mountjoy 5–0, a win that catapulted me straight into the semi-finals against Jimmy White. And when I sauntered off with the first frame, the stargazers were marking me down as a formality. Trouble was, someone must have messed about with the planets.

On a good day, Jimmy is a magician. On a bad day, he gives the impression of being bored by the game and not caring about his performance. No one can dispute that he has enormous flair and natural talent, and as he matures as a person it would be nice to assume that his professional pride will grow, as well.

This time, the packed Kelvin Hall crowd were treated to a spell of Jimmy at his peak. He settled well, dashed confidently around the table, was unaffected by my first-frame win, and deservedly swept in front by three frames to two at the interval.

My long potting, so often the main feature of my game, dropped way below its usual standard, but I still managed to stick with Jimmy up to 5–5, with just the final frame to play.

I had a gem of a chance to clinch the match in the closing stages, but I fluffed a fairly easy shot using the half-butt, and Jimmy nicked the game. There was no time left for a recovery mission, and Jimmy went on to beat Cliff Thorburn in the final and achieve his biggest professional conquest to date.

On the debit side, it was my first crash in a major tournament for more than ten months. I knew it had to come. But what bothered me most was that I was literally lost for words. Barry and I had never rehearsed a loser's speech! There is no point in pretending that I wasn't disappointed to lose to Jimmy. Yet I knew that one defeat in a small tournament could do me no harm.

Some people might have even welcomed the result. There was a small school of thought that believed snooker could become boring if I continued to win everything. I'm hardly a paid up member of that school. I'm greedy. I'd win the Grand National, the Boat Race and the Cup Final all in the same year if I could. Winning is a drug. It gets into my bloodstream. Some players, of course, can't perform at all unless they are topped up with booze, or chain smoke until it's pouring out of their ears. I don't do either. A glass of cold water and the will to win are enough for me.

Thorburn crushed Higgins 6–2 in the other semi-final, which was remembered more for a Higgins flare-up in frame four than for the quality of its snooker. Higgins protested that the scoreboard had robbed him of five points, and he was correct. Yet again the promoters had failed to employ a recorder to make an official note of every point.

Higgins had potted a red-green and a red-black to earn himself twelve points, but the scoreboard gave him only seven. Even then the error wasn't spotted straightaway, and it took someone from the BBC to draw it to Higgins's attention.

True to form, Higgins flew into a rage. He was extremely abusive to everyone in sight, including the embarrassed referee. As you'd expect, all his ranting was in vain, and the score remained unaltered. Like so many people I find it increasingly odd that when a controversial incident occurs in snooker, Higgins is usually the man in the middle.

Thorburn carried his brief, new-found form into the final and rushed into a commanding 4–1 lead before Jimmy rallied well to win eight frames in a row and take the match 9–4.

With two tournaments completed, the rest of September was spent slaving at exhibition matches and covering more miles a day than a Yorkie driver. From Port Talbot on the Monday, I travelled some three hundred miles to the Fiesta Club at Stockton on the Tuesday, a further two-hundred-and-fifty miles to the Lakeside Club in Camberley, and then one hundred miles to Abingdon on the Friday. In all, I clocked around a thousand miles in six days – a serious handicap I've had to work under from having a manager who only recently agreed to take geography lessons!

I crawled through Abingdon at twenty miles an hour so that everyone could have enough time to see my Porsche. For once, I felt like Jack the Lad. I felt like going on an ego trip – a big-headed idea that soon backfired on me and brought me down to earth.

As I drove into the car park, my electrically-controlled headlights were set in an upright position. Several people came out from the club to meet me and I switched off the engine. The headlights dropped back into position just as I wanted them to, but as I began locking up I suddenly noticed that they were rising again ... and dropping. They kept going up and down, and there was nothing I could do to stop them.

As you'd expect, a crowd soon gathered and a handful of kids kept running around shouting, 'Come and see Steve's headlights. He can't stop them going up and down!'

A fault had developed in the relay system and after much sweat I eventually got them to stop, but not before I was emphatically cured of showing off for the rest of my life.

Next day, I took a deep breath and flew to Ireland for the annual Coleraine Classic, a one-day tournament that brought together Terry Griffiths, Dennis Taylor, Kirk Stevens and myself.

To brighten the hall, the organisers had put flowers everywhere. Dennis thought it was Mother's Day, and on one occasion the referee stepped back so far that he almost got lost in the jungle. Bees and wasps zoomed all over the place. One massive wasp landed on my shoulder while I was playing Dennis, and the referee was so concerned for my safety that he gave it a vicious karate chop with the side of his hand. The wasp died instantly, and I almost went with him!

Obviously stung into action by all this, I slammed Dennis 3–0 in just thirty-one minutes in a semi-final match that was scheduled to last five frames. I was truly buzzing, and breaks of ninety-four, seventy-five and fifty-seven were as sweet as honey....

Terry had to battle much harder to kill off Kirk 3–2 to reach the final, in which I was never extended to beat him 4–0. This meant I had come through the tournament without dropping a single frame.

My mad routine brought me back to Manchester on the Sunday when I ended up roasting Higgins, which I always find more than satisfying when playing in his home town.

By now I had accumulated £10,000 in seven days, and even Barry was satisfied. He said I could take Monday off to sleep.

The wasp in Dublin reminded me of the large fly that tormented Tony Meo and me for seven frames during an exhibition match at the Sports Centre in Swindon. It buzzed about under the shade, dived on to the balls and at regular intervals swooped across the table.

Tony and I tried hard to concentrate on our shots but, just as we were about to play, the pest would come in low, like an enemy bomber, and escape into the darkness before we could get our ground forces into action.

After failing to bring him down with the butt of our cues, a recorder's clipboard and several outstretched hands, the referee stopped the game and went in search of a more powerful weapon. Shortly afterwards he came back with a large can of deadly fly-spray, guaranteed to kill like poison gas, and waited in the dark to ambush the pest once it came on its next assault. As it did so, and with play still held up, the referee went berserk on the trigger, firing incessantly until a thick grey mist began to swirl under the shade, leaving the table barely visible from my bunker in the corner.

Tony was standing up at the time, and as the mist steadily engulfed him, he spun round and round on the spot and then, to enormous laughter from the crowd, he dropped to the floor and lay flat on his back. It was a very funny moment, but as he stumbled to his feet and prepared to take his next shot, the fly, now hit and out of control, made yet another daring raid on the table.

I stood up, switched on my radar, spotted him zooming in over my left shoulder, raised my lethal interceptor and grabbed him! For a time I felt him wriggle and fight, so I gripped him harder. Then, satisfied he was crushed, I raised my hand high over the table and he dropped to the cloth to a chorus of groans. The enthralled audience had obviously enjoyed the aerial battle as much as the snooker.

7

Surviving a Hurricane!

Part of my 1981–2 *Daily Star* contract included a new series of six challenge matches in which I would play other selected leading professionals all over the country. Terry Griffiths and I launched the series at the Leisure Centre in Ebbw Vale, where I beat him fairly comfortably by five frames to two.

Returning to Ebbw Vale brought back memories of my previous visit to the steel town, where I was literally brought to a standstill by a phantom fart-blower lurking in the audience.

I was playing a top amateur in a local competition sponsored by Courages. I had just potted a red, and was preparing to pot the brown, when someone doing a Heinz Beans commercial could hold back no longer.

Biting my tongue, and staring straight at the table, I tried desperately hard to keep a serious face. I thought it would be wrong for the world champion to be seen laughing. But, just like the phantom fart-blower, I couldn't hold out for ever. Irishman John Smyth was the referee, and once he starts laughing, he can't stop. As soon as he saw my face, he burst out into a huge, unstoppable roar, and the whole place cracked up. Of course, Ebbw Vale is Doug Mountjoy's home town, but I don't think it was him!

From sampling some Welsh Rarebit, I left for a ten-day tour of the

North-East and Scotland where my new diet was to be double helpings of Higgins tripe.

Barry employs a highly-organised promotional team that accompanies me to all the major tournaments and exhibition matches. We put up a stand that sells every imaginable snooker accessory, along with wall-posters, pictures and books.

Several weeks before my northern tour, Barry secured the exclusive rights for his stand to be present at every place I played. But sparks flew on the very first night when Higgins walked in and charged across to the stand and scattered posters all over the floor. He didn't like it because we were selling Alex Higgins posters, and he wasted no time in announcing to the crowd that he would autograph only those posters that were bought from him. I kept well away. Having to face Higgins on the table is enough without going out of my way to confront him in the foyer.

The promoter then telephoned Barry, threatening that if he didn't back down, Higgins would walk out. He also said that he might be forced to withdraw the promotional rights. Barry told him not to be so stupid – the contract was legally binding, and he could just as easily pull me out. Barry also said that as he had the exclusive rights, he could object to Alex selling his own posters as it caused a breach of contract.

The flames finally died down when Barry agreed that Higgins could sell his own posters, but remained adamant that we would go on selling everything we wanted to from our stand.

As expected, Higgins blew his top, and he continued to be obnoxious right through the ten days. He gave everyone hell. We stayed at the same hotel, but I made certain we kept well apart. I saw him only when I had to – at the snooker table. To be candid, the only time you get a good word from Higgins is when he is winning and, although he played fairly well, I won the tour comfortably.

This was the first time on the road for the promotional van, and I enjoyed a good laugh with Don Tate, who manages it, and his assistant, Ann. If nothing else, it was a nice change to sign proper posters instead of tiny slips of paper. I must say that when we set up the promotional team it was not done to make lots of money out of the fans. Far from it. Barry and I are delighted to see it break even. To be frank, we believe it provides a much-needed service and brings a more professional touch to exhibition matches. So far it is the only travelling stand of its kind, although it has now been extended to cover matches involving Tony and Terry, as well as mine.

I was offered the choice of being chauffeured from venue to venue in the same car as Higgins or driving on my own. I said that although I would get terribly tired driving alone, I'd prefer to listen to my tapes than listen to Higgins.

It was a devastating tour. In most cases I played both in the afternoon and the evening. I drove in convoy with the promotional van, which helped a great deal because then I didn't feel entirely on my own. In many ways it was exciting to be on the road, travelling as a team, eating and sleeping in the same places and planning our routes together.

Altogether I played in Edinburgh, Glasgow, Inverness, Aberdeen, Stirling, Irvine, Dundee, Newcastle and Carlisle. And in almost every case, we played to packed houses both day and night. Often I would spend four to five hours on the table and then set out on journeys of two to three hundred miles at two o'clock in the morning. On one occasion, after a full day at Newcastle, I went out for a meal, got to bed at two and was up at six to drive three hundred miles to Inverness in time to play at two o'clock. This was typical of the gruelling schedule.

All through the tour Higgins remained totally obnoxious. There is no other word to describe him. But I took great care that his moods should not get under my skin and spoil my enjoyment.

Yet, despite the many agonies I suffered, I would go through it all again – provided, of course, the right type of money was put up for me. And I would do it with Higgins, only next time I would take my own driver so that I could sleep in the car while I made those terrible journeys.

From all the television, radio and newspaper coverage I keep receiving, it seems I have ended up something of a national celebrity, and many people keep asking me whether I find it difficult to cope with being in the public eye so much. To be truthful, I don't. I seem to thrive on it. Being a celebrity is exciting, and I love excitement. But perhaps to some extent I can understand why Higgins is forever throwing a tantrum. I don't believe he has the right temperament to cope with people and fame. That is why you find him doing so many impulsive and outrageous things.

I pocketed £9,000 for those ten days on tour, which was cheap at the price. If I do it again, then I'll want to be paid more. By my standards it was extremely hard work. Not just the driving and constant playing, but having to put up with my opponent for so long.

I left Scotland feeling like a drenched haggis. I was physically and mentally drained. I needed a month to recuperate and even Costa del Clacton looked attractive at the time. To make matters worse, I had picked up a rampant stomach bug, and I made more runs in seven days than Botham makes in a season! It was the type of stomach complaint you would normally expect after a month in Bombay.

Still, the show had to go on. I was booked to play Higgins at Bath and while he had his favourite alcoholic drink at his elbow to sip between shots, I kept knocking back the kaolin and morphine.

For once I was looking forward to playing him. At least, I knew I'd be quick! On one shot I felt a sudden rumbling in the stomach and I thought, 'Oh, no, it's going to be a monster.' There were four or five reds left on the table, and Higgins had just finished off a fifty break. Within minutes I had completed the quickest clearance of my life. Then I rushed outside to rapturous applause and proceeded to complete another clearance, only this time without paying customers!

At one stage my stomach was so bad that I considered hiring a Portaloo and booking a caddie to carry it around Wentworth for me during a *Daily Mail* golf tournament for snooker players.

Thorburn, Higgins, Spencer, Stevens and Reardon were also there. Barry came, too, and kept calling himself Corals. He made Thorburn the 3–1 favourite and filled his brown bag.

There is no doubt that Thorburn stands head and shoulders above every other snooker player at golf. After the match he made a speech, in which he said: 'At least, it's nice to win something this year!'

Higgins became so frustrated with himself in the closing stages that he erupted into a slanging match with his caddie. Higgins insisted on taking a certain club to play an approach shot to the eighteenth, when the caddie, who knew virtually every blade of grass on the fairway, advised him to take a different one. Though having to suffer the blunt end of Higgins's tongue, the caddie still went away with the last laugh. Not only did Higgins pay him for the round, but he was also paid by the organisers. Higgins was livid when he found out, but he never got his money back.

Golf's main attraction to me is that it provides an opportunity to walk around in the fresh air among pleasant surroundings, and know that I'm not going to have anyone coming up to discuss the quality of my shots. Many people have said that the golf bug will bite me in the end. Never! I enjoy the game solely for the relaxation it offers and I can't see myself ever taking it seriously. I approach it in the same way as I approach horse-racing. Going to Cheltenham and having a private box right on the finishing line is my idea of relaxing in luxury. And if I back a winner, then it's a bonus, and usually followed by a mild heart attack!

My real idea of luxury golf is cruising around on a buggy on a hot summer's day with a crate of cool beer on the back, and getting slowly merry from tee to tee. Then smashing the little ball all over the course and occasionally venturing into places where golf balls have never been before.

Thorburn is a highly skilled golfer. He treats the game deadly seriously. Unlike me, he really wants to play well. And I believe his immense devotion to golf might have partly accounted for his swift and definite decline from the snooker scene.

I am convinced that no player, no matter how talented he might be, can succeed to the same degree at more than one sport. Time and concentration are of paramount importance in practice and playing, and only a fool will argue that they can be divided up equally to obtain the same results. A player who dabbles in several sports must be in danger of ending up a master of none.

By all means use a secondary sport for relaxation purposes. That can only be good, both physically and mentally. But you must make sure it goes no further.

In Thorburn's case, he might also have resented the public's tame response to his year as world champion. Compared with the euphoria that surrounded my victory, and then followed me through the year, Thorburn was almost forgotten overnight. Mind you, he didn't help his cause by returning to Canada for a couple of months after his world championship victory.

I believe this bothered him, and I certainly didn't help his recovery when I ground him out of sight in our titanic world championship semi-final. Perhaps if he had overcome that hurdle, he might have pulled himself together and become more determined to re-establish himself. As it turned out, he just continued to slide lower and lower down the helter-skelter.

Ever since I first met him, he has always given me the impression of having a chip on his shoulder. No matter whether he's winning or losing, he has that peculiar knack of looking morose. This has baffled me, because when he's away from the table he can be a great laugh – a very funny man. Sometimes I feel that he might be worried about the flaw in his technique, knowing that the time has long gone for him to practise and correct it. For a perfect cue action, a player's arm must be absolutely straight at the moment of contact, but in Thorburn's case the cue goes round in an arc, which causes him to miss many potable opportunities. At one stage his confidence was sky high. Now it seems to be at rock bottom, and it's going to take a considerable time for it to return and make him the feared force he once was.

Some players also find it difficult to handle success, and I reckon Thorburn might just come into this bracket. Dennis Taylor and Eddie Charlton are two more who find it hard to come to terms with winning, and I can understand why.

I remember lying in the bath before the final of my first Corals UK victory and suddenly realising that I could win. It sent a shiver down my spine. It was quite frightening. But once I had accepted that I could win, and more importantly that I could handle it, then I just went out and did the job – and got Barry to prepare the speech!

I felt a lot of pressure during those championships. It was my first definite breakthrough into the big time. Fortunately for me, that type of pressure has always reared itself away from the table, never during a match. Once I arrive in the arena I am perfectly relaxed and I can clear my mind of everything but the game in hand. My entire attention is focused on winning.

Every player must feel pressure from time to time. It would be absurd to say otherwise. But there is a huge difference between trembling in the hotel and trembling at the table. If you're going to be sick, then try doing it in the loo, not on the cloth!

8

Captain Courageous

Before my eyes were fully accustomed to the Wentworth sunlight, I was back indoors for the State Express world team championships at the Hexagon Theatre in Reading – a new venue for the event, with first-class facilities for players and supporters.

In all, seven teams – England, Wales, Australia, Canada, Northern Ireland, Rest of the World and the Republic of Ireland – lined up to compete for prizes totalling £40,555, with £12,000 of it being divided among the three men in the winning side.

After my run of success in the months before the international, I was given the very special honour of leading my country. Not bad for a player who couldn't even win a place in the side the year before!

John Spencer and David Taylor completed our team and this puzzled a lot of people who believed that Tony Meo and Jimmy White should have been preferred. At that time, Jimmy was the only player who had beaten me, admittedly in a small tournament, in the six months since the world championships. And John Virgo, having won seventeen of his twenty frames for England the previous year, understandably had his large batch of supporters shouting his claims.

Ironically, to prevent such confusion, it had been decided much earlier in the year that the team would comprise the world champion (if English, of course), the United Kingdom champion, and the English champion. Just to wreck these well-laid plans, I went off and won the lot and qualified for all three places. But as the rules stipulate that it must be a three-man team, it was then agreed that the remaining two places would go to those who did best in the world championships.

Neither Spencer nor Taylor progressed particularly far, but they did better than the rest, and so automatically won their places in the national team. Tony Meo was terribly unlucky because he got as far as Spencer, but was not selected because he won fewer frames.

This was the first year that the world cup was really well organised, and a truly international occasion. It was also the first time that I had heard such a tremendous roar for a team rather than for a player. It didn't matter who was at the table, the fanatical support was always the same.

There was nothing tame about the matches. It was more of a drama series than a question of sport. There couldn't have been more tension if I had written the script myself. To full houses, and in front of millions of viewers, I felt like Scott from *Thunderbird*, as I constantly came to the rescue when all seemed lost.

Being captain, I was bound to get the spotlight as I always played last, but no one should under-estimate the excellent contributions from Spencer and Taylor. Yet, it was nice to know that if a match went to a tie-break, then I would have the job of going out to win it. In all, I won tie-breaks against Australia and Northern Ireland, a semi-final thriller against Canada, and the vital tie-break against Reardon in the very last frame of the tournament to clinch victory and cause an epidemic of laryngitis back in the valleys.

Recalling the tournament in more detail, England didn't play on the opening day, so Barry literally put me in the cart, touring the streets of Reading pulled along by two magnificent shire horses in a promotional venture for Courage, the brewers.

I was in the cart later that day, too, when the tip fell off my cue while playing Higgins in an exhibition match in Worthing. To complete the show I had to borrow a cue from the rack to play the last few frames.

I had put the tip on just three days before the international, and I was far from happy with the way it was playing. Most professionals prefer a firm tip, but it must also have a certain amount of resilience.

Mine was especially hard, and with absolutely no 'give'. I thought seriously about taking it off and replacing it in time for the match, but I was caught in a dilemma and couldn't make up my mind what to do. When it eventually fell off, I decided that the 'man upstairs' was looking after my interests and that even He didn't think it was a good tip to use.

As it turned out, I went into the first day of the international with a tip that was not played in at all. The best I could do was tap it gently against a few snooker balls to simulate some wear and tear. David Taylor was far from amused when I told him, realising immediately that it could cost him £4,000 as part of the winners' share-out. This again indicated the spirit of team-play. In any other tournament David would have been thrilled to see me turn up with a brand-new tip.

Of course, Taylor, Spencer and I knew one another well, which was hardly the case in the Northern Ireland camp. Their three players stayed at different hotels, and when Higgins arrived in the dressing-room and saw Tommy Murphy standing there, he said, 'Who are you? What are you doing here?' Higgins evidently thought Tommy was an autograph-hunter.

Whenever David Taylor or Spencer were at the table, I went out and joined the audience and literally quivered in the back row. For the first time I realised how traumatic it must be for my father and Barry when they come to watch me play. I have never been so nervous. For once, sitting on the sidelines, I had absolutely no control over the balls on the table. I felt terribly frustrated and helpless.

In one frame against Reardon, Spencer potted a brown and nearly went in-off and I almost collapsed in my seat. I let out such a loud gasp that everyone looked around to see what was happening, and when they saw me they knew straightaway how badly I was suffering. My hands were sticky with sweat and I was literally shaking.

I was hardly in a better frame of mind for my first match against Australia. While travelling from home, a lorry suddenly swapped lanes on the motorway and dragged its back end along the side of my Porsche, leaving an ugly scar on the passenger's door.

As the driver was Spanish, I didn't make much impression with my Romford 'volley', so I still had lots of wrath to unload when I went out to play Eddie Charlton in our first game.

One of my best shots against Eddie was a long, difficult yellow.

The problem was not so much potting the ball, but gaining perfect position behind the green that was lying on a side cushion. I was offered the choice of playing a safety shot or of going flat out for the game. I fancied the shot a lot, went for it, and screwed-back half the table to roll up smoothly behind the green. I then proceeded to pot the green and followed up with the brown to win the best of three frames.

My victory over Charlton meant that I had forced a tie-break for England. But before I had time to smile, I found myself badly adrift and in need of a snooker on the blue. I succeeded in getting one, but thought Eddie would easily find his way out of it. But to everyone's surprise, he missed the blue, I mopped up, and England scraped through. Phew! Too close for comfort.

Life was no easier when we faced Northern Ireland in the quarter-finals. This time, it was Dennis Taylor who caused the trembles. A solid break of seventy-four helped him beat me two frames to nil, which prompted yet another of those awful one-frame play-offs. Dennis was now attempting to win his third frame in a row, so the odds were stacked against him for a start.

With England's survival at stake, I was determined to play hard. I put my head down, applied maximum concentration and clinched the tie-break to lead England nervously into the semi-finals, which immediately threw Barry into a frantic panic. Having lacked any confidence in England going this far, he had booked me for a six-hour exhibition match at Telford on the same day as the final. In a desperate flap, he telephoned the promoters and said that Higgins would deputise for me in the exhibition match if England got through. A brilliant and instinctive idea – until Higgins and his Northern Ireland colleagues also reached the semis! Barry promptly rang the Samaritans!

England faced Canada, while Northern Ireland played Wales, the title-holders for the previous two years. David Taylor carried our flag, facing a thirsty Bill Werbeniuk in a fascinating opener, with Bill soon needing a pint of lager to cool him down after a fiery disagreement with senior referee John Williams. Bill blew a fuse after John had penalised David for a foul shot, and then changed his mind and allowed it to stand.

Bill eventually lost the match two frames to one, and he was still simmering when he returned for his evening game against Spencer.

All of a sudden he now began arguing that the cue ball was different from the one that was used in the afternoon session.

The organisers told Bill that he was wrong, but to pacify him they brought out an entirely new set of balls which again did him no good. He went down for the second time, on this occasion two frames to nil. In reacting to Werbeniuk's protest, Spencer sarcastically suggested that the cue ball had JS stamped right through it, like Brighton Rock.

On reflection, I am sure that both Bill and John were caught up in the electric atmosphere that gripped the place, although John did admit that the ball was playing in a peculiar way.

Thorburn agreed with Werbeniuk's views and lodged his own protest as captain of the Canadian team. Yet, when everything had cooled down and returned to normal again, he must have wondered how he ever allowed himself to become involved in such a trivial matter. On a more rational note, I believe the ball started to behave so oddly because the atmosphere changed in the arena. I remember it began to rain outside and I'm convinced that the damp air worked its way indoors, soaked the cloth, and altered the playing conditions.

All sorts of atmospherical conditions can affect a snooker table. One of the most common is when a table is brought in for an exhibition match after being stored in a cold room. In a short time, the atmosphere will warm up in the hall and condensation will form on the slates. This dampens the cloth, and in minutes you can be playing in entirely different conditions. Just like a thunderstorm hitting a cricket pitch. The run of the ball will change dramatically in such situations, with the ball reacting altogether differently.

Such subtle changes in playing conditions present yet another extreme challenge to the top professional, because his ability to adapt to new circumstances is put to the test. Having said that, all the world's best players should have the experience to notice the changes creeping up on them and be able to handle them without much trouble.

Naturally enough, the paying customers don't want excuses trotted out when things go wrong. A player can't suddenly put his cue down and say that it's raining outside and that this has ruined his performance. They'd lock him up. All the customers want are century breaks and lots of snooker skills. They have seen the full works on television and expect the same high standard at their club, no matter how bad the table might be, or how tight the pockets are playing.

At some clubs, the first words I hear are, 'You'd better watch the top right-hand pocket. It's a real tight one. We have a lot of balls missed in there.' And there are those who gloat: 'You might do it on the telly, but you won't do it here.'

By the end of the night, a good player should have worked out the speed and run of the table, and the balls should go in without much fuss. On a match table, where the pockets are expertly cut, a player should have much less difficulty in potting the balls, and should become accustomed to the speed of the cloth within a few minutes.

Kirk Stevens kept the Canadian flag flying briefly with a 2–1 win over David Taylor, but I tore it down once and for all when I beat Thorburn by two frames to nil.

Wales accounted for Northern Ireland, as laid out in the form-book, but only after an unexpected struggle that stretched to yet another of those fascinating tie-breaks. Ray Reardon rose to the challenge this time and dominated the frame with a fifty-one break, sinking Dennis Taylor by ninety-three points to thirteen.

So, with Northern Ireland knocked out and Barry happily up off his knees, Higgins left for Telford and David Taylor, John Spencer and I set our sights on a titanic battle against the formidable Welsh trio of Reardon, Mountjoy and Griffiths.

Corals immediately chalked us up as short-priced favourites. This was something of a surprise, as we all knew the Welsh players would fight tooth and nail to keep the trophy which by now was virtually their own.

Back in the mid-seventies, when Reardon ruled the world as champion, one of the few players to run him close was John Spencer and, in many respects, both of them slipped down the ladder at the same time. If anything, Reardon has maintained the better standard, and there are signs now that he is working a lot harder at his game in a positive effort to re-establish himself. He has obviously missed being at the top, and with the money getting bigger and bigger, his appetite for the game seems to be creeping back. Despite his drift into the shadows, Reardon has still managed to cling to his reputation. He has kept his supporters with him and he receives a tremendous reception wherever he plays.

The two former giants of the table met in the opening match, when a good start was essential to both teams. Unfortunately for us, Spencer succumbed by two frames to one, before I levelled the score, beating Mountjoy convincingly by two frames to nil. The scene was set for an unforgettable final.

Sadly for us, David Taylor was not at his best on the last day, and lost both his games, the first to Griffiths and the second to Mountjoy. But, just as Taylor faded, Spencer picked the right time to recapture a great deal of his old sparkle. He called on all his vast experience and cunning, and produced a magnificent one-hundred-and-three against Griffiths to keep us in the game.

So, with England trailing by three frames to two, it was again down to me to beat the determined Reardon. The tension was red-hot, but I somehow managed to remain absolutely ice-cool. Curiously, I found the excitement rather stimulating, particularly having to walk out representing a team rather than just playing for myself. The roar I received was incredible. I had more people rooting for me than I could ever remember. Of course, a large contingent of Welsh supporters helped to charge the atmosphere, constantly shouting out words of encouragement to their players that I couldn't understand.

For once, Reardon offered very little resistance, and I played particularly well to win the best of three and find myself in the third tie-break of the tournament. At least, I was well used to them by now. Earlier on, Reardon had beaten Dennis Taylor in a tie-break to earn Wales a place in the final, so it was very much the showdown of the tie-break champions.

As it turned out, I raced off with a break of 43, but then amazingly missed a rather simple red into the middle pocket which would probably have set me up for a winning break. Urged on by his supporters, Reardon replied with a break of 43 which suddenly broke down when he missed a difficult, yet potable, last red into a top corner pocket. A pot in that situation would certainly have put him in a perfect position to clean up the colours.

When he struck the ball, a few people sitting directly in line with the pocket started cheering, which usually means the ball is on its way in, and I felt a lump come up to my throat. But this time they had misjudged the line, and the ball just caught the knuckle and stayed invitingly over the hole. Right out of the blue, I was presented with the easiest possible clearance to win the tie-break and lead England to their first ever World Cup triumph.

Though I say it was basically an easy clearance, I still had to obtain perfect position on the colours, and with the red directly over the hole, my job was made slightly harder because there was no scope to create an angle. Somehow I had to find a way of directing the cue-ball on to a colour. This I did, and then continued to take all the colours up to the pink, and the match was safe.

Smiling as usual, Reardon held out his hand, and Taylor and Spencer quickly came out of the audience to congratulate me. I was delighted. And the noise was deafening. When I looked across the hall, the three Welsh players seemed terribly downhearted. This, I suppose, was only natural when you realise that they had played together for a long time, and had now been deprived of an international hat-trick.

With the cheers still ringing in my ears, I accepted an invitation to challenge John Mann, the British pool champion, in a best-of-three-frame match in front of the cameras for Independent Television's World of Sport.

I have no great love for pool, but I agreed to play, and when I got to the hall I was besieged by a number of people practically begging me to bet on myself against their champion. I asked them sarcastically: 'Oh, you're a bit short, are you?' And I offered to pay them there and then. I knew full well that Mann was favourite. To be approached in that way was not entirely surprising, because most pool players think and talk in terms of money.

The first frame was absolutely disastrous for me, with Mann tying me up in knots with lots of tactical play. I did much better in the second frame, mainly because I decided it was pointless trying to beat him at tactics.

Unlike him, and other pool players for that matter, I couldn't be bothered just to roll the balls over the holes. Instead, I potted my lot in double-quick time – including the white and the black! This meant, of course, that I had automatically lost the frame and the match.

Many people couldn't believe that I had lost to a club pool player, and the more suspicious even thought the match was fixed. I took a fair amount of criticism afterwards, although I realised that most people don't understand the difference between snooker and pool.

Pool is a tremendous pub game, but nothing more than that. There is no scoring, so there are fewer rules than in snooker, and they are obviously much simpler. As a game of pool is usually operated by coins, it is ideal for pubs, and the table is so small it can normally fit comfortably into a back room.

As I see it, there are too many boring tactics to make pool widely popular. Snooker has tactics, but the game is constantly on the move. Pool is nowhere as fast or as skilful. And it is easy to understand why so many snooker players can adjust to pool, whereas very few pool players can switch to snooker. The high degree of accuracy demanded by snooker proves way beyond them.

When snooker players do try pool, they prefer the type called Straight Pool, the game featured in the film *The Hustler*. It is more a game of positional skill than actual potting, and provides an opportunity to try combination shots and plants, which appeals to me much more than rolling balls over pockets.

English pool is also very different from American pool, in which the balls and pockets are quite enormous. In English pool, the pockets are so tight that the game inevitably ends up as a bore.

One of the main tactics that makes pool such a drag to me is that instead of an experienced player going flat out to pot all his balls on the table and then try to pot the black, he will laboriously roll them over the holes and cover up the pockets, hoping, at the same time, to place the black in a favourable position for his final attack. If a player goes for the lot and fails, and leaves one ball on the table, then he's snookered for life. In some respects, I suppose pool can be interesting, but then so can Ludo.

Pool is very much a gambling outlet. Players don't accumulate points as they do in snooker, so it is essentially a game for just those who are taking part and certainly not for spectators. The only time I dabble in pool is when killing time at an hotel, although I did once reach the quarter-final of a Pontin's competition and won £25 and a free holiday. To win it, was real torture. I forced myself to spend a whole day just sitting and watching how the game was played and trying to learn the tactics.

Of course, pool is strictly an unfair game. Penalties for certain shots are ridiculous, particularly the one involving the black which, if accidentally potted, can cost you the match with your very first shot. Though, as it's a coin-operated game, I suppose for some people, it's not such a bad rule, after all!

Straight after the televised pool, I flew to Belfast for the Northern Ireland eight-man invitation championship at the Ulster Hall and promptly upset the locals by removing their hero Alex Higgins by five frames to two.

I then beat my arch rival Terry Griffiths 9–6 after being level at six each, and moved on to face Jimmy White in the twenty-one-frame final. Jimmy had beaten Cliff Thorburn 5–2, and Doug Mountjoy 9–8.

In front of a jam-packed crowd, Jimmy enjoyed a flying start, capturing the first two frames before I hit back to lead 3–2 at the interval. The match continued to swing to and fro until I looked sure to win at 9–7, needing just two more frames to take the £5,000 prize. But Jimmy dug in when I least wanted him to, and retaliated extremely well to win the last four frames in a row to whip the title from under my nose.

This was Jimmy's second tournament win over me in quick succession, and the newspapers inevitably jumped at the chance to plaster large headlines that the Young Pretender was now ready to take my crown. Personally, I never regarded it as a major tournament and found it extremely difficult to motivate myself. It had neither the glamour nor the excitement of those large, televised English tournaments that never fail to get my adrenalin going. Besides that lack of incentive, I felt I had been a bit open in my play, just as I had been against him in the Scottish Masters. My safety shots were below par and I didn't put him under any pressure. I vowed that the next time we met, I would play an entirely different type of game. Still positive, but taking fewer risks.

It is only when a player has lost a match that he turns it over in his mind and realises where he went wrong. There is usually too much going on during a match for him to spot his tactical errors and alter his approach. And in any case I suppose at that stage he still believes he's playing the right type of game and can pull the match out of the fire in the end.

Altogether that Irish visit was a bitter disappointment. Shortly before my match with Higgins, I did a programme for Ulster Television and I was signing autographs in the street outside the studio when a group of kids came along and tried to attack me. They were a bunch of ten-year-olds who had nothing better to do than roam the streets as a gang.

According to some English papers, I was punched in the face, had a broken leg, a skull fracture, and almost choked when the cue was pushed down my throat. In reality I felt like Kenny Dalglish with my ankles tapped. Later on, I was told a taxi driver telephoned the story to the newspapers and dressed it up, possibly to get some Guinness money.

The most degrading thing they did was to spit in my face. A friend was standing by to drive me to the Ulster Hall, and I managed to jump in his car and slam the door before the kids could do any real damage. Then they lashed out with their hobnailed plimsoles and kicked a few dents down the side as we drove off, just to give us a warm Irish welcome.

From then on, all the same, I took no chances. A plain-clothes policeman went with me everywhere. On the day following the street incident, I was walking down the stairs at the Ulster Hall when someone with an armful of empty bottles accidentally dropped one and it smashed at my feet. It was a complete accident, but some of the English newspapers got hold of it again and built it up into a huge story about someone having deliberately thrown the bottle at me.

The whole Irish incident left an unsavoury taste in my mouth. A lot of well-wishers apologised on behalf of the Northern Ireland people, but I was still glad to get back home to England. Although violence and tension abound in that area, sport is the one thing that breaks all human barriers and keeps people sane and together. I very much hope it will stay that way, as I always look forward to visiting the Emerald Isle, whether North or South, as the support there for snooker is almost fanatical.

A similar situation exists in South Africa, and I have strong feelings on the subject. The British Government persist in trying to stop our sportsmen from competing in that country, yet have the audacity to trade every day at the top business level. There can be no grounds for such double standards, and until the British Government can set a fair and proper example, they have no moral right to expect the country's sportsmen to stand firm and do the job for them. I love playing snooker and I would hate to think that a few meddling politicians could put pressure on the game and cause unnecessary problems.

My first defence, and the strain begins to show. The Coral UK at Preston.

No danger! In any event, better bet Davis. . . . Retaining the Coral UK championship.

Hi folks! Welcome to Vegas. A long way from Plumstead. . . .

The dynamic duo go dicing in dollars.

Did we know something about the 147 a few days before.

Jubilation at Porthcawl, seconds after Barry's million-dollar putt.

In the pink. Now just one shot from the magic 147.

History is made and the crowd go wild. Moments after the 147.

I'm still in a daze as Allan Deal, chairman of Riley's, presents me with the balls used in the historic frame.

Have a break. Have a Lada.

Clowning around on Tiswas.

With Sally James during one of her legendary interviews.

Dan Hegarty reconstructs the 147, only this time in coloured flans! And he didn't miss a shot.

Having a flantastic time. Wish you were here!

In at the death. The last Tiswas, and Meo came too.

Terry Griffiths and me, still smiling in yet another major final together. The Benson and Hedges Masters at Wembley.

More like a Grand Prix driver at the Chelsea Flower Show. Collecting the Benson and Hedges trophy.

A visit to the Leisure Industries factory at Bideford in Devon.

Watching the manufacture of a Steve Davis Pot Black Table.

Relaxed, but still trying to be kingpin.

Potting Brownies on Blue Peter.

Before the off. Team-pairs poised for the Courage pro-celebrity ten-pin bowling tournament in Leeds.

We've bowled them over! With Steve Neff after striking out the opposition – even if Patti Boulaye did beat me.

Pot Black final. With Minister of Sport Neil Macfarlane and Alan Weeks after beating Steady-Eddie. Yet another one for the mantelpiece.

'I think it's over there. . . .' A Courage golf day at Southampton. Barry and me, and our caddies Radley and Robbo.

Tough luck . . . Barry completely misses the ball in front of the TV cameras, and Radley and I can't help sympathising.

Visiting Hudson's store in Birmingham during the launching of my first book.

Another successful defence. Retaining the Yamaha Organs International Masters in Derby.

'Where's the money?'

I must have played well – even dad said so!

A Super Star of the Year, no less – official.

9

Critics KO'd at the UK

With the Irish tournament over, the Coral United Kingdom championships were just around the corner and I began to feel the excitement gradually welling up inside me. This was the first of many major titles I would have to defend through the year, so I was determined to halt my disappointing run, and to put a lot more effort into my play.

Being a champion is all about consistency, concentration and ruthlessness. They must be the big guns in my armoury. As far as I am concerned, money will never be the main motivating factor, and I think my willingness to play in exhibition matches all over the country emphasises this point more than anything else. I may be well paid, but in an exhibition match I play for pride, not for cash. Being satisfied with my performance is more important to me than any sum of money, and I believe every sportsman should think in the same way, provided he is professional enough.

At exhibition matches, I also keep in mind that the customer has paid for his seat and that there is an obligation on me to try my best to give him value for money. That's partly why I always stay behind, when an exhibition match is over, to play a few trick shots which everyone seems to love. This part of the show also gives me an ideal opportunity to talk to the audience from the table, and to share a joke and a laugh. Not every professional thinks this way – Higgins and White, for example, have a dislike for trick shots and rarely play them.

By rights, I should have put the record straight against Jimmy three days after our Irish final when we were booked for a challenge match in Southend as part of a three-day snooker spectacular organised by Steve Davis Promotions Limited.

The booking was confirmed on 3 June, exactly five months before the date on which we were due to play, and there was never any suggestion after that that Jimmy would pull out. A few days before the match, however, Barry decided to telephone Sportsworld for them to confirm that Jimmy was definitely coming, and he almost fell out of his chair when they claimed they had no knowledge of the engagement, and said that Jimmy was due to play in a charity match that night for Henry West, his manager at the time of the booking.

What Barry found strange was that Jimmy had turned up for all the other dates confirmed in a letter to Henry West – so why not this one? This left Barry wondering whether Sportsworld didn't fancy Jimmy playing me so close to the championships, but he said, 'Oh, no, they wouldn't pull a stroke like that on us, surely?'

Now we were stuck. At very short notice we had to find a top-class player to bail us out. In the end, John Virgo agreed to play, joining Doug Mountjoy, Higgins, Meo and me in a series of exhibition matches that clearly gave enormous pleasure to large and appreciative audiences. If nothing else, the event enabled me to have yet more important match practice shortly before the championships.

Willie Thorne was my first opponent in the Coral UK. He was still recovering from two broken legs sustained in a Go-Kart accident three months earlier and hobbled around the table in elastic bandages, but I had no intention of offering him any mercy. Anyone who has seen Willie Thorne at his best will know that only a fool would underestimate him, because he is such a vastly talented player. Feeling in good form, I made two century breaks and played some extremely satisfying snooker to beat him 9–2.

Next came Bill Werbeniuk, and I was never stretched to outplay him by nine frames to five. This brought me on to the semi-finals and the dramatic showdown with Jimmy White, which the Press and the public at large had built up into bloodbath proportions.

As the game came closer, I psyched myself up tremendously hard. I was determined to win. Some people had even started to think that

Jimmy was the better player – influenced, no doubt, by a few fairy stories in the cheaper Fleet Street comics! I concentrated one hundred per cent on the game, shutting everything else out of my mind. I was so psyched up to win, that I decided I wouldn't allow him one chance to get back in the game if I could help it. I knew that if I lost, it would be a massive stumbling-block. It was vitally important that I should win, and the bigger the margin, the better for me.

In principle, I don't believe in going around boasting about my ability and my achievements. I prefer to let my performances at the table do all the talking for me. For some peculiar reason, parts of the British Press always seem on the look-out for new names which they like to build up into overnight stars – and then proceed to knock down twice as fast.

Just for the record, I annihilated Jimmy by nine frames to nil. I raced to an 8–0 lead in the afternoon session, and took just twelve minutes to finish him off when we returned to the table in the evening. Altogether, I made five breaks of sixty-plus, and my ninety-seven was the highest of the match. Jimmy's best was thirty-six.

On the day of my match with Jimmy, the *Sun* newspaper published a ridiculous article which claimed that I wasn't the best player in the world. After I had beaten Jimmy 9–0, the *Daily Star* leapt at the chance to retaliate, and said on their front page, 'Yes, he is the number one – and so are we!'

Barry showed me the *Sun* article just before I went out to play. I don't know whether he had it in mind to psyche me up, but if he did, then he left it a bit late. I was already more than prepared for the job in hand. To be frank, I was quite annoyed that, even after I had won virtually every tournament in the previous twelve months, there were still some people around who doubted my ability.

For obvious reasons, I did my best to hide my true feelings. Barry, however, was far more outspoken. Expletives powered from his mouth when he read the *Sun* article. It was the first time for me to hear that the *Sun* newspaper didn't have parents! In a terrible rage, Barry held up the paper and attacked the article as a 'cheap shot'. Though the words in the piece were attributed to Jimmy, we both knew that he didn't say them, because all Jimmy wants to do is play snooker. That's what he is good at. He doesn't get involved in silly back-biting and slagging other players. Barry got really steamed up over the 'ghost' responsible for what was said.

My own feeling was that the article put even more pressure on Jimmy, just as his manager had done earlier on when trying to build him up into a superstar. Jimmy is basically a nice bloke and should be left alone to do his job – playing snooker! Not surprisingly, as I walked from the table after beating Jimmy, the grin on Barry's face was wider than I had ever seen it.

My chance to put the record straight came in a television interview with David Vine shortly after the match. I trotted out a few home truths, all of them intended to help Jimmy. I took a swipe at his so-called advisers, not at him. In fact, Jimmy's father was the first person to congratulate me for what I said about the way Jimmy was being mishandled, and this meant a lot to me. Though Jimmy and I have little in common away from the table, we have a definite mutual respect for each other as players. There is certainly no animosity between us.

Terry Griffiths had beaten Tony Meo in the other semi which prevented an all-Hearn final and so robbed Barry of a big winning bet. Barry was confident that Tony and I would meet in the final, and he had obtained some very attractive odds with Corals several weeks before the championships.

The final, spread over two days, was the best of thirty-one frames, and I envisaged a tremendously hard game and psyched myself up to the limit for it. As it turned out, I finished the first day leading by an incredible thirteen frames to two, and needing only three more frames for an important personal victory. Even then, with the championship staring me in the face, I continued to psyche myself up for the sprint to the line. That's how much it meant to me to keep that title.

I didn't take long to wrap the match up next day, winning the tournament by an overwhelming sixteen frames to three. And I not only kept my crown, but won the match with a whole session to spare, just as I had done the previous year, when beating Alex Higgins. In this second UK victory I dropped only ten frames out of fifty-three, which pleased me a great deal. It was further proof of my consistency, which I consider so important.

Of course, we all know now that this was the start of a long run of close matches between Terry and me over the months to come, when we became talked of as the Borg and McEnroe of snooker, although in strict terms, there is absolutely no resemblance between Terry, the perfect gentleman, and the boisterous American. Right through the year, Terry and I were to figure in almost every final that mattered, although I must say that in all those tournaments covered nationally by television, the ones that really count, being in the public eye, I always went away with the honours.

I should like to correct all those people who think that Terry has suddenly improved overnight, that he's found some magic formula and closed an imaginary gap on me. The truth is, there was never such a gap in the first place. Terry has always been a remarkably good player.

When playing him, I know I can't take any liberties. If he's let off the hook, then he'll come charging back. How can I ever forget my first world championship experience when I led him 7–1, and he fought back to 10–10? To hit back like that is the sign of a great player. What's more, Terry takes pride in his work, which can't be said of every player.

Having seen Terry off early, I found myself with an hour or two to kill, and for the first time in my life I started tapping the keys of a piano, which I found in the corridor near my dressing-room.

All of a sudden I felt an urge to play, and the newspapers soon latched on to it and I was swamped with letters from people wanting to teach me. In the same way as I used to unwind by playing the Space Invaders, learning to play the piano offers a great way to relax. A perfect retreat from the snooker table – like having a house in the country!

Ever since I started playing in major tournaments, Barry has helped me take my mind off the game by coming to my dressing-room during the intervals. We talk about everything except the match going on at the time. We have a good laugh and it eases the strain. If I've just come through a tough session, the last thing I want to do is brood over it.

I was so delighted to retain the UK trophy that I really let my hair down and dived into the champagne. I put away so much, that when I ran into a door-handle and smashed a finger, I felt nothing. I was numb from the head down. We had a fantastic party back at the hotel, and I ran around slipping large ice-cubes down the back of everyone in sight. This was the time to release all the enormous tension that had built up inside me over the weeks leading up to the championships. You might say I was set free! Before going to bed, I stuck my aching finger in a jug of ice, and when I awoke next morning, all I could see was a black, throbbing mess where my nail used to be. The finger was so sore, I had to hold it up straight to ease the pain.

Winning a tournament sponsored by Corals means a lot to me personally. I shall never forget that they were the first major company to take an active interest in my career. I regard them as friends, and recently they reinforced their interests in snooker when signing a contract guaranteeing £260,000 for the United Kingdom championships over the next four years.

10

Graduating with Honours

From soaking myself in champagne at Preston, I was soon literally wallowing in milk. Gallons and gallons of it passed through my lips while I prepared for a television commercial with jockey Jonjo O'Neill and darts champion Eric Bristow.

Day number one was spent filming me potting the black, with Higgins calling out 'A lotta bottle' in time with the music. Day number two was taken up with Jonjo, Eric and me pretending to sink glasses and glasses of milk and desperately attempting to sing the punchline together.

Then came the crunch. We were asked to take two swigs of the real stuff, as the film had to be genuine. So we went on filming ... and filming ... and filming. In every 'take', we knocked back pints and pints of the white stuff, and much as I like milk, I must have drunk a cow dry.

To loosen us up in front of the cameras, someone suggested we should drink a few glasses of wine, and I am still not sure whether this improved our performances or ruined them. Looking back at the cock-ups later on was great fun. Definitely the best part of it! Considering all the hard work everyone put in to make the project come out perfect, the commercial itself was over very quickly.

My acting ability was streched even farther a month later when

I joined Gareth Hunt in a coffee commercial for Nescafé. I started filming at nine in the morning, struggled on until three next morning, and went home with the milkman!

I found it impossible to manage the punchline – 'This is the one to pot!' Just saying it in normal circumstances among friends, and with no cameras around, is easy enough. But in those false conditions, surrounded by cameras, my tongue just couldn't come out with the words.

The funniest moment came when I had to pot a red and allow the cue-ball to end up behind the pink which was lying in the middle of the table. At this point, Gareth was supposed to say, 'When you have a world champion around for coffee, you want to give him the best. . . .'

Unfortunately, when I got down to play the shot, I messed it up completely, snookering myself on the pink by the green. I then had to rush around the table to Gareth, who cleverly changed his lines and whispered: 'When you have a world champion around for coffee, you want to give him the best because he's bloody useless when he's supposed to be on the pink and not the green!' Needless to say, this part of the film was dumped in the bin, but after much practice we did eventually get the shots and the words right before another day came around.

Sometimes at home I sit back and feel truly grateful to snooker for all it's done for me in opening the doors to the wonderful world of showbusiness. Just through snooker I have been able to mix with celebrities other people would give their right arm to meet.

Immediately after the United Kingdom championships, I teamed up with Frankie Vaughan in the very popular pro-celebrity snooker tournament run by Yorkshire Television. Frankie is a smashing chap, but he admitted to me that he was terribly nervous about the competition.

As you would expect on occasions like these, it is very much the snooker player's job to calm his novice partner, but Frankie was an impossible case. He was so nervous that when he tried to play a red ball at the bottom of the table, with the white on the top cushion, he developed such an awful twitch that as he struck the white, his cue shook so violently that it thumped against the green and sent it speeding across the table. The referee rightly called out 'foul', and Frankie panicked so much that he hurried after the green, literally picked it up and tried to put it back on its spot. By the third match, he had settled down a bit, but our chances of winning had long since disappeared.

Appropriately, I suppose, it was the Gaffer, Bill Maynard, who won the event, partnered this time by Terry Griffiths. Bill was winning it for the third year in a row, and the professionals are now queuing up to pay him to be their partner next time round.

Commentators John Pulman and Dennis Taylor joined in the spirit of things with many amusing remarks about the players and the situations they found themselves in.

Dennis told a real funny story about a visit to a nightclub while still wearing his evening suit after a match at the local hall. He was standing just inside the door of the club, minding his own business, when a man five times his size grabbed a glass of beer and threw the lot over a woman sitting nearby.

The woman got straight to her feet and rushed up to Dennis, shouting her protests and asking him what he was going to do about it.

'What do you mean?' queried Dennis, bemused and terrified.

'Well, grab him. Kick him out! You are the bouncer, aren't you?'

Being knocked out of the pro-celebrity at an early stage meant I could spend more time recording a Christmas show with those amazing comics, Eric and Ernie.

A mock snooker arena was set up at Teddington Studios, rent-a-crowd was brought in, and the idea was that four sketches of me playing Eric in the 'world championships', Morecambe style, should be spaced out through the programme. Barry came along, too, as an extra. He's always wanted to get into films.

Of course, Eric was supposed to put me off my shots, I was to look ridiculous, and Eric had to win. The script laid down that I had to keep a straight face at all times, but I found the pair so funny that I just couldn't stop myself from giggling out aloud.

At one point I completely cracked up. It said in the script that when I played my shot, Eric should cough and distract me. Then I had to turn round and look terribly angry. But on seeing Eric's blank face, I burst out laughing and, although this part was obviously cut from the show, I can still see my shoulders going up and down when I watch it on the video.

In the first scene, Eric licked the tip of my cue and I missed my shot, leaving him badly snookered in the jaws of the pocket. Only the difficult massé shot could get him out of this one, but, unseen by viewers, I stepped forward and played it for him. All through the programme, Eric was shown at the table carefully cueing up and preparing to play, although in fact, I took every shot for him. In reality he could just about pot a ball if it were left in a direct line two inches from a pocket.

Both Eric and Ernie are extremely professional performers and knew exactly what was needed to make the show a stunning success. Eric reckoned the most encouraging sign was when all the scenery workers and camera crew came to a halt and sat down and watched the show being put together. They are so used to seeing rehearsals, and become so blasé about them, that the action has to be special to make them stop and listen.

In another hilarious scene, I was all prepared to pot a red when Eric distracted me again. I was supposed to flare up, only I couldn't stop laughing. Eric then arrogantly went to the table and potted three reds in one shot. I enjoyed myself so much making that show, and I was so relaxed, that the snooker just oozed out of me. I have rarely played better.

It was one huge laugh from beginning to end. They dropped the cue on their feet, chalked their fingers and did all sorts of ludicrous things. To finish the show, they stuck me in a tatty raincoat and a flat cap and had me to jump around doing a stupid dance.

I have always been a great admirer of their act, and I can remember as a kid being glued to the television set, watching their shows, particularly over Christmas. So to be invited on a programme of such class was a rare privilege, and yet another door that snooker had opened for me.

While I was filming with Eric and Ernie, excitement was growing over my chances of doing well in the BBC Sports Personality of the Year award, which was just a few days away. After my good performance in the televised UK championships, lots of people kept telling me that I couldn't have timed my challenge better, and that this must have encouraged people to vote for me. Terry Griffiths gave me a wonderful plug on television and the votes, apparently, came flooding in.

Before I actually went to the studio in Shepherds Bush, I had no preconceived ideas of how well I had done. But when I arrived and was called aside and told that I was definitely in the first three, I was convinced I had won. So without wasting a second I began to work hard on what I would say when Frank Bough called me up to receive the award.

In fact, I concentrated so hard on my speech that when they announced I was second, it came as a complete let-down. Ian Botham, after his fine Test series against the Australians, had obtained more votes than me. I was bitterly disappointed and, worse still, I knew I hadn't prepared a runner-up speech!

Yet, despite this disappointment, I was still delighted to finish second in such an important national poll, and I was very grateful to all those people who had taken the trouble to write in for me. If nothing else, it proved that I was a very popular person in thousands of homes all over the country, and that pleased me a lot.

It was also a great achievement for snooker in general. It was marvellous to see that it had risen to such prominence in sport and was being enjoyed by so many people.

Yet another honour came my way when I was listed as one of the Radar Men of the Year and presented with a certificate to commemorate the occasion at the Savoy Hotel in London.

I was nominated alongside such heroes as Trevor Lock, the policeman in the famous Iranian Embassy siege, and Phillip Olds, the policeman shot and crippled when trying to stop a robber. From the world of sport, Alan Wells, the athlete, was also there.

Though I felt proud to be in the company of such people, I still thought honours of this dimension should be reserved for those who perform genuine acts of courage or give their lives freely while carrying out important public duties. Quite naturally, the biggest cheer was given to the two policemen, with Trevor Lock receiving a standing ovation.

A few months later, Pye Colour Television voted me their Personality of the Year, and I met royalty for the first time when introduced to Princess Michael of Kent at the awards ceremony. Jan Leeming, the BBC announcer, was voted their female 'personality'. Susan and Barry came with me, along with Tony Meo, and I enjoyed another excellent day of stardom.

For a whole month up to Christmas, I was inundated with radio and television appearances, many of them on the children's programmes, which I enjoyed immensely.

From wearing huge, fluffy bunny's ears on Crackerjack, I graduated to 'potting' twelve real, live Brownies on Blue Peter. To give the impression of a snooker table, a large green carpet was laid out on the studio floor, along with six 'pockets', and I had to race around with my cue and pretend to pot the Brownies. I had to play over their heads, and the Brownies had to somersault across the table and roll into the pockets. And I had to pot everyone of them in the time it takes to play the Pot Black theme tune, 'The Black and White Rag'.

Compared with these fun programmes, going on Question of Sport was like taking a Mensa test. I joined Daley Thompson in the Gareth Edwards team, but from the way I fluffed the answers I might have been a spy from Emlyn's side.

I double-faulted straightaway. When shown the studio picture-board, I was asked to identify a foreign tennis player by his colourful armbands. Beaten by the service, all I could say was that he must have lost his match with broken wrists!

Even when snooker appeared on the 'What Happened Next?' section, I crashed again. I was shown a recording of Doug Mountjoy breaking off to start a frame, and after the cue-ball had struck the pack, two reds rolled off to the side cushions.

'What happened next?' asked David Coleman. I was snookered! Of course, I should have remembered that both reds amazingly returned to their original positions to form the perfect triangle again.

To answer questions of that sort in front of staring television cameras is not as simple as it seems. In most cases, my mind just goes blank, although I can normally answer a few at home, and other people have said the same thing happens to them.

However, my general performance can't have been too disastrous, because they invited me back for a second try, and I decided that if the questions proved a little difficult, I would wave my arms around and try a joke or two. Billy Beaumont and Sue Brown, successful cox of the Oxford boat, had the job of keeping me on an even keel. Thanks to a few snooker questions, I did much better, but I still felt in the mood for a good giggle, and messed about a bit. Strangely enough, the biased Romford panel of my mother, father, Barry and Susan gave me low marks for gross over-acting, although I later received more than a hundred letters from people saying how much they had enjoyed the performance. Some of them even had the cheek to suggest that I should be appointed team captain.

I used my Question of Sport season ticket for a third time when asked to join Steve Ovett in Billy's team. The trickiest question came in the warm up when Billy asked me if I knew where and when a black boxer went to the toilet in the ring after winning a championship. I couldn't work it out, and Billy said, 'Crufts, 1962!'

11

Flans and Chips

Nothing but the best will do for Barry and, true to form, he laid on a magnificent champagne breakfast to make sure my autobiography went off with a fizz. So many people turned up from newspapers, magazines and radio, that Barry had to send out for extra bacon and booze, and organised two sittings in order that everyone could be accommodated.

I am delighted to say that the book sold so well that it went into its fifth reprint just six weeks after being published, and the Pan company were so determined to buy the paperback rights, that they outbid several keen rivals. To help promote the book, I attended signing sessions in Romford, London, Birmingham and Manchester. They were all well attended, and I welcomed the chance to sit and chat with people who were looking forward to reading about my life and how I grew up in the game.

Russell Harty grabbed a copy and I was invited to appear on his television programme. It was my first chat-show, and I've never been so nervous in my life. It was a different type of nerves from what I'm used to in snooker. This was the fear of venturing into the unknown. I had no idea of what to expect. In snooker, I get nervous when looking forward to a game, particularly when I'm waiting to be announced. The tension always starts in the dressing-room where the time ticks away slowly as I wait for the call. What made it worse with Russell Harty was my knowing that the show was going out live. There was no margin for error. But once I actually sat in the chair and the grilling began, I felt much better. Having a responsive audience definitely helped. Once I had said a few things and they had laughed, my chair actually stopped shaking. I felt at ease.

Eventually we moved on to a snooker table that had been specially brought into the studio. Obviously, once I had my hands on a cue, it was like being back at a club doing an exhibition match. Russell had asked me to play a few trick shots to round off our chat, and the first one worked so well that I became a bit ambitious and attempted a difficult one-handed screw-back into the middle bag and botched it up.

Rather than try it again, I moved on to the tour de force – potting the black out of Russell's mouth. Earlier in the day, I had been given a victim to practise on, and everything went perfectly to plan. I knew full well, of course, that success in practice might be encouraging, but being able to produce the goods on the night was all that mattered in the end.

In the full glare of lights and cameras, and to a background of chuckling and laughter from an audience who were enjoying every minute of it, I asked Russell to lie flat on his back across the table, while I proceeded to place a lump of chalk in his mouth, and then delicately balanced the black ball on top of the chalk.

Satisfied with this part of the preparations, I then placed another piece of chalk on the table-edge, close to Russell, and this time balanced the white on it. The idea was to cue the white ball off the chalk, knock the black out of Russell's mouth and pot it in the left-hand pocket at the other end of the table, and it went in like a dream.

The audience let out a tremendously warm cheer and they were clearly as thrilled as I was that the shot had gone so well. To fail would have meant a terrible anti-climax. It was such a great finish that Barry admitted to me later that he was so excited, sweating in the front row, that he felt like jumping up and rushing out to shake my hand, just as he did in the world championships. Russell was definitely as nervous doing my bit of snooker as I was doing his bit of chat, and I'm certain he'll never again allow a ball to be potted from his mouth like that one.

For one of my *Daily Star* challenge matches leading up to Christmas, I was booked to play Higgins in York. Higgins had just come out of hospital.

Newspaper reports quoted Higgins as saying that he was off his food, had lost weight and was drinking too heavily. He was on the brink of a nervous breakdown and needed a complete rest under medical supervision.

Unfortunately for Alex, I was in top form that evening and I slaughtered him. Then, when the match was over, Higgins suddenly went up on the stage and said he wished to thank his supporters for all the loyalty they had shown to him. Taking the microphone, he said: 'In the words of Muhammad Ali, my greatest hero, I want to say that I can return! I shall return! I will return!' Some people started clapping, and I joined in. I couldn't believe what was going on. It was hilarious.

I was down to play him again the next night, in a *Daily Star* sell-out in Batley. As I drove to the club, snow started falling heavily, and radio reports warned that parts of the motorway were already impassable.

Having deliberately set out early, I arrived at the club with ninety minutes to kill. As we were not sure how Higgins would react from his hospital spell, Barry sent Tony Meo up from London by train to stand by. Referee John Smyth, crying out for ski dogs, skidded up from London by road, taking six hours in atrocious weather.

Everyone arrived on time, except Higgins. There was no sign of him. After a few telephone calls we were told he was stuck in traffic, so Tony and I filled in with an exhibition match while we waited for Higgins to arrive. In time he did, and we played nine frames, in which I thrashed him again.

This time my problems were not so much on the table as on the road. The snow was piled high, and I didn't fancy being stuck in Batley all night, sleeping on a settee. I didn't have a booking next day, but Tony was in a terrible flap because he was booked on a flight to Italy for a holiday.

Using some wire-mesh and shovels we managed to dig our way out to the car. I had just got inside it and was revving up, when a little kid noticed my window was down and slung a snowball that burst all over me.

Batley is situated deep in a dip, and with steep hills on each side.

I thought we needed a miracle to reach the summit. But, skidding all over the place like a rally driver, I crawled to the top on my side, revving violently all the time, and probably doing less than a mile to a gallon. John Smyth also made it in the blizzard behind me, and when we all reached the top we met a JCB digger and its driver agreed to clear a path for us towards the motorway. There was no one else on the road.

On reaching the junction that led to the motorway, the JCB driver decided to leave us and pointed to oblivion, reminding me of pictures of explorers in the Arctic. So as the JCB disappeared into the white night, Tony and I screwed and slithered our way towards the motorway. Somehow, we made it and waited for John Smyth, who eventually came zig-zagging out of the storm.

The roads were appalling and John Smyth did several dances. After filling up at a station in Outer Derby, we reached Birmingham at around three o'clock, when it started to rain, and by the time we arrived in London at eight, the snow had cleared altogether. I dropped Tony at his home and he quickly rushed off to Heathrow in a state of panic, only to find that his flight had been delayed and there was no cause for alarm. He eventually arrived in Italy fifteen hours late.

Being involved with Tony in the snow like that brought back memories of the evening we played in Kent and a blizzard kept us in town all night. The promoter invited us to stay with him and his family, and we found they had two spare beds – one near the fire, and the other suspended by four chains from the ceiling. Tony and I decided to toss a coin. He won and chose to sleep in comfort near the fire, leaving me to do spirographs all night, swinging from side to side and going round in circles like a sailor in a storm.

As usual, Christmas came early in Romford with Barry and me deciding to dress up in Santa Claus outfits, along with the beards, to hand out presents to our 150 guests. We held the party in Barry's office and took care to invite only those who meant something to us personally. Having dished out the gifts, we called everyone together for some ridiculous games, most of them inspired by Barry himself.

We started off by staging the first ever push-peanut-with-nose world championships. A copy of my autobiography, signed by Tony, Barry, Vic and me, was put up as the prize. The guests were split into teams of girls and boys, but Susan appointed herself shop steward and said it was degrading for the girls to be seen down on their knees in crude positions, and went on strike. So Barry and I banned them.

One man was so determined to be champion that when we reached the final he kept hitting the floor so hard with his head, as he pushed the peanut along, that he broke his nose and it wouldn't stop bleeding.

To end a marvellous night of fun and games, we put on the country's first ever Snooker Mastermind. Barry and I picked out six of Romford's alleged walking snooker encyclopaedias, which included my dad, Les Coates, Robbo and Bobby Lazarus, and asked them all to sit in a line while Barry and I played Magnusson.

What our victims didn't know was that Don Tate was waiting outside in a flan-flinger outfit, and when they got a question wrong he would rush in and bury them in custard pies. I would signal his assault with a loud blow of my whistle. When my dad's turn came, he was sitting quietly in front of us with a massive cigar, like a brush handle, sticking out of his mouth.

'Who won the 1979 world championships?' he was asked.

Dad went silent. I could see his mind was blank. Then, as he turned the question over in his head, he eased the cigar out of his mouth, just for a split second, and Don leapt in screaming, 'Too late!' The flan splashed against dad's face, and the whole place erupted.

Les Coates answered his question correctly, but was still flanned. The last question went to Robbo, a very funny man and the bookmaker's best friend.

'Who won the 1981 world championships?' he was asked.

Not attempting to answer, Robbo dived towards Barry, grabbed his arms and held them tightly behind his back, shouting for Don to flan Barry. Don moved towards Barry, but just as the flan left his hand, Barry ducked and Robbo took the full blast flush in his face.

All this hilarious flanning proved the perfect dress-rehearsal for the real thing when I was asked to go on Tiswas and found myself on the receiving end for a change – and loved it.

Barry brought Katie to the show, and David Brimacombe brought his young daughter, Sarah. In the days leading up to the programme, Katie became awfully worried about receiving a flan in her face. Barry assured her that nothing would happen, but when we arrived and went backstage, who should step out in front of little Katie, frightening her out of her mind, but the real, nasty flan-thrower, raring for practise! If that wasn't enough, seconds later Dan Haggerty burst from behind some scenery and planted his foot against her stomach, pinning her against the wall. And she loved every minute of it!

Tiswas invited me back again two weeks later for the last show of the series when a host of clowns, including Spike Milligan and Frank Carson, were among the guests. Katie was 'too busy' to come this time, and flans were 'no longer her scene'.

On my first Tiswas, the producer dreamed up a game called The Flanaha Trophy. All the flans were the colour of snooker balls, and I was supposed to represent the world snooker table of 1982. They handed me a huge coat with large pockets, but they didn't tell me which flans went in the pockets and which ones went in my face. I just stood, cringed, and took a pasting.

Unknown to me, a big bucket had been filled to the top with some disgusting brown gunge and while I was being bombarded with flans, I heard a frantic voice guaranteeing my escape if I leapt into the bucket.

'Great idea,' I thought, and jumped in!

The wretched sticky stuff was well above my knees and my new pair of shoes were ruined. I was drenched to the skin in thick, brown slime, and I just couldn't stop laughing. I was just carried away by the fun of it all.

Barry and Tony Meo came with me the second time, and I had the pleasure of lifting the lid and flanning the shocked and terrified Tony. Worse still, as Tony was getting to his feet, a horrible kid crept up behind him and rubbed the flan all over Tony's face and through his hair, leaving him in a terrible mess.

To add some weight to the programme, the producer decided to bring on a massive African elephant, led up by Ted Moult. But the animal became more and more excited as he waited his turn in the wings and suddenly backfired with the most deafening noise, the gust of wind almost bringing down the scenery.

Fate had placed Barry close up, and in a direct line with the elephant's bum, and he sprinted away like Seb Coe as the most revolting smell filled the studio and sent us all scampering off for our gas-masks.

* * *

Before all the top snooker players can welcome in the New Year, they must first take part in the BBC's fascinating *Pot Black* series which is always televised at the Pebble Mill studio in Birmingham over three days in the last week of December.

My two previous attempts to win this trophy had ended in disaster, so I was determined to do better this time. I approached the event with an entirely new attitude. I decided to play as open as possible and hope for that vital bit of luck that is always needed in tournaments of this sort. It is essential to hit form right from the start. There is no time to warm up or work your way into a competitive frame of mind. If you don't click straight away then you can book an early taxi.

I enjoyed a lot of luck while beating Dennis Taylor in my first game and when we reached the lift together, I pressed the button and the doors opened immediately. Dennis is a sharp comic and he said, 'If I'd pushed that button we'd have been here ten minutes waiting for it to come down from the tenth.'

My next game, against Reardon, had all the twists and turns of a good thriller, with Reardon finally outgunning me on the black. I slayed Eddie Charlton in the following game, and this earned me a semi-final place against the defending champion, Cliff Thorburn.

Semi-finals are contested over two frames, with the player achieving the best total score going forward into the final. I was so far behind in my first game against Thorburn that I looked like going out altogether. With just two reds left on the table, I was a colossal 72 points adrift and still waiting to hit the cue-ball in a straight line. Thorburn then amazed everyone by missing an easy black off the spot, and I potted the last two reds and all the colours to end the frame just 27 points in arrears when, in fact, I should have been plucked and roasted.

The following frame was different in every respect, and it highlighted yet again the sudden and decisive way in which snooker's fortunes can fluctuate from one game to another. After just one safety shot, I set off on a match-winning break of 91 which left Thorburn glowering in his chair and in need of several snookers when he eventually dragged himself to the table. It was a startling turnabout, and I coasted home without a hitch by 113 points to 24, and took the semi-final by an aggregate score of 139 to 97.

Eddie Charlton won his way through from the other 'semi' and in a final over two frames, I comfortably beat him 2–0, and by 167 points to 98, to ruin my record in *Pot Black*.

As I've developed a reputation for warming up quickly and winning most of my opening frames in big tournaments, some people were puzzled as to why I had not done better in *Pot Black* in previous years. However, with its sudden-death format, *Pot Black* doesn't exactly suit my style of play. In those other competitions, I know that if I don't succeed straightaway, there are other frames to come when I can get on top. Such an opportunity doesn't exist in *Pot Black*, so I'm forced to take more than the average number of risks.

Right through this latest *Pot Black* tournament, Dennis Taylor was at his funniest, constantly cracking jokes with the audience. He had us in stitches, and the players were confident that he had done more than enough to win the Personality award, presented every year by the BBC.

'Here he goes again for the Personality award,' was probably the most over-used sentence of the whole three days. Then the organisers shocked us all by presenting it to Ray Reardon.

For a change, I wasn't sick on New Year's Eve, bringing an end to a two-year run. I desperately wanted to stay sober as I was due to board a British Airways Jumbo-jet with Barry next day for an important business flight to Australia.

Promoter Stephen Lewis had cabled us from Perth, saying he wanted to stage a sponsored snooker spectacular involving Australia's hero Eddie Charlton and myself in a series of head-to-head confrontations in front of large crowds.

Stephen reckoned it would be the richest-ever contest of its kind, with a world record of $100,000 coming my way for twelve matches. He hoped three of these could be played in Sydney, and if all went according to plan, they would be held at the city's famous Opera House. He explained that one proposed venue in Perth could seat up to eight thousand people, although I thought the balls would seem rather small to those straining their eyes in the back row.

Before we could embark on such an ambitious tour, Barry thought I should first be introduced to the Australian snooker public, so a series of television and radio interviews were arranged, along with photographic sessions for the Press.

To kill time on the flight, which took an endless twenty-two hours, I played cards with Barry until our eyeballs hung out, and we drank champagne in the first-class area – the only way to travel for people with legs as long as mine, when every spare inch is a gift against cramp.

The plane stopped off in India, and when Barry looked through the windows he was horrified at the huts and the poverty that surrounded us. I had played in the Bombay Open so I had seen those sights before and really believed that no one could appreciate such poverty existed unless witnessed at first hand.

The plane also stopped off in Tahiti, but I slept right through the break and the cleaners had to brush around my feet as I lay back, flat out, dreaming of world championships. I missed both the landing and the take-off.

It was midnight when we eventually touched down in Perth, and as we walked from the plane all the people who greeted us were bronzed and in shirt sleeves – a startling contrast to what we had left behind at Heathrow.

My first impression of Perth was that everyone seemed to be living in the lap of luxury, with large houses and even larger swimming pools. A long way from Plumstead Common! But before I could get carried away with the splendour of the place, a chap came up to me in a tee-shirt emblazoned with the words, 'Come to Perth – six million flies can't be wrong.' I soon discovered what it meant. There was a personal fly for each one of us.

Drained from jet-lag, Barry and I had planned a few hours of sleep before we set out on our PR work, but when we felt the warm air touch our faces and saw the swimming pools, sleep quickly took a back seat and we dived in.

This was the first time for me to see Eddie Charlton in his own country after he had had a drink. About fifteen of us were sitting around a private pool when Charlton said, 'Let's go down to the nightclub.'

It was two o'clock in the morning, and no one else was keen to go. So we took a vote, and Charlton lost, fourteen to one – and we went to the nightclub! That's the type of hold he seems to have on his own people. We reached the nightclub at 2.30, and it closed at three! So we moved on to another house, another pool, and ate our way through a stack of steak sandwiches, and then ended up watching the sun rise again.

From Perth, we flew on to Sydney, and yet more swimming, more saunas and more Press conferences. My jet-lag legs were like sticks of jelly.

Before finally flying out of Australia, my twelve-match, 132-frame tour was provisionally arranged for the first two weeks of April, but we soon found that there was insufficient time to complete the deal and the trip was postponed until early in July.

With time running out, Barry and I flew on to Las Vegas to try to get the Americans interested in the game. We wanted to test the ground for a small exhibition match in one of the big hotels, as we both realised that the game could go sky high if it caught on over there.

Again we thought of making up on lost sleep before committing ourselves to a long grind of talks, and two uninterrupted days of gambling. We carried our bags into the hotel, looked out on the city's mass of twinkling lights, shrugged our shoulders and decided to put in some practice straightaway and learn the rules of Crap. We quickly found a chap who agreed to teach us the game in exchange for a regular supply of booze, and as he became progressively drunker, he started to spill his beer down the shirt of an angry dealer.

Fun at the casinos provided the perfect break from a round of talks with the tough Las Vegas businessmen. Unfortunately for us, the promoters in general were not impressed, and thought the game would attract the wrong type of customer. They believed the public at large would associate snooker too much with pool, which, I'm afraid, has left a bad image there, and this is the first and biggest obstacle we have to overcome. To be frank, snooker has taken a long time to shake off its poor image in Britain, but I think the game is far too great for the Americans not to accept it before long.

Of course, it is a brand new game to them. It has no roots in America, but it would be a crying shame if it went untried. I'm convinced that if those promoters came to Britain and saw the tension and excitement the game creates when played at top level, they would love to take it back, and that it would reach the same heights that golf has over there. The skills of snooker are far superior to those of pool, and I'm sure that once they realise this their interest will grow and the game will take off and be signed up by one of their multi-billion television stations.

We certainly haven't given up hope, and we are encouraged by murmurings that a small tournament is now highly likely to be staged as an experiment in Las Vegas. We also have fresh plans to explore the possibilities of taking the game into San Francisco.

Our sole reason for being in Las Vegas was to open their eyes to snooker, but no one in his right mind who found himself enveloped in such a carnival of gambling could fail to find some time to play a game or two. I was an instant success on the Big Wheel of Fortune, winning a thousand dollars on a 10–1 shot with just one spin. Spurred on by my luck, Barry and I went back and asked to have $100 at 20–1, but they wouldn't let us. We had obviously broken the house limit.

Later on I became involved in a poker school, and I won again. I also won at dice. All this winning frustrated Barry, who had lost a few notes. He definitely got the needle and accused me of not being a proper gambler. He reckoned that to be a proper gambler, you had to lose. All I said to him was, 'Don't go away, this sucker is just off to cash his chips again!'

To complete a fabulous round of entertainment we saw Dionne Warwick and Frank Sinatra in concert, and had a tremendous time in every way.

On a less comfortable note, every time I touched a door-handle I found a nasty shock shooting up my arm. I developed a mental block about it and even when I returned to England it stayed with me for two or three days. I would go to open a door and then pull away at the last moment.

While in Vegas we visited the video games exhibition where some friends of ours had a stand. The whole town was packed with thousands of representatives from practically every video company in America and Europe.

But along with the representatives came an army of dubious young ladies, all flying in from other States. One newspaper reported that around 1,200 of them had been stopped at the airport and sent straight back. The local police chief, defending his actions, was quoted as saying that he had sent them packing because that type of business should be strictly reserved for the local girls! Yes, Vegas really is a crazy place.

One thing is certain, now that I'm back, I have no desire to go round looking for casinos in which to waste my money and time. I'm too much of a bad gambler for that! When in Vegas you do the same as everyone else, and for me, that's where it came to an end.

We were told in Vegas that Heathrow was closed because of snow on the runways. Barry immediately threw up his arms and groaned, 'Oh, what a choker! Now we'll have to stay here with all this good food and the gambling.' As it turned out, one runway was cleared and we were able to take off on time.

Before leaving Vegas I must have drunk a whole bottle of champagne. I can remember feeling terribly dizzy as the plane took off. It was my idea of a pleasant nightcap to guarantee a good sleep before arriving in London and going straight into the Lada championships at Oldham. Even then, I still woke at five, the changes in time having messed me up again.

When the news came through about the snow at Heathrow, I was worried I might not arrive back in time for the Lada. It called for a desperate dash and, though I made it in the end, I was hardly in good physical or mental shape for a major tournament. After the sizzling sunshine of Australia, we were back on ice at Heathrow, having raced round the world and experienced three time changes. My head spun just thinking about it.

From Heathrow, the whirlwind swept on. I rushed off to Barry's home in Essex, collected my cue and some clothes, and the same night drove up to Oldham to clock in for the Lada. By now, I was nothing more than a sleep-walking Zombie masquerading as a world champion. But the show had to go on. . . .

12

History, Euphoria and the Magic 147

My only real practice for the Lada came on a Leisure Industries miniature table at the Toy Fair in Harrogate. A few hours before my first match, I fell out of bed and drove to the Yorkshire town to fulfil a long-standing engagement, knowing full well that I could spend very little time there before having to drive back again. I must have been in good form because while still half-asleep, I almost made a complete clearance on that small table, which proved to be a great omen for the marvellously historic moment that was only an hour or two away.

Arriving back in Oldham, I managed fifteen minutes of practice on the match table before changing for my quarter-final game against John Spencer. It was six in the evening, and I was extremely tired.

For the first four frames I really struggled to hold on to John, and I was more than pleased to be 2–2 at the interval, with neither of us having produced our best snooker. Then came frame five, and probably the most memorable moment of my life....

In the following pages I have tried to reconstruct in diagrams and words an historic frame of snooker. Fortunately I have not had to do it entirely from memory, because I have been able to watch the frame shot by shot on video. It has been extremely difficult, even so, to achieve complete accuracy in the diagrams, since there is no film showing the table from above. Perhaps one day someone will think of mounting a camera directly overhead. . . .

In the diagrams the red balls are lettered, from 'A' to 'O', in the order in which they were potted; the colours are numbered according to their values; and the dotted line shows the path of the white ball after contact. I should also point out that the 'top cushion' refers, as always, to the end of the table where the black is, not to the top of the diagram.

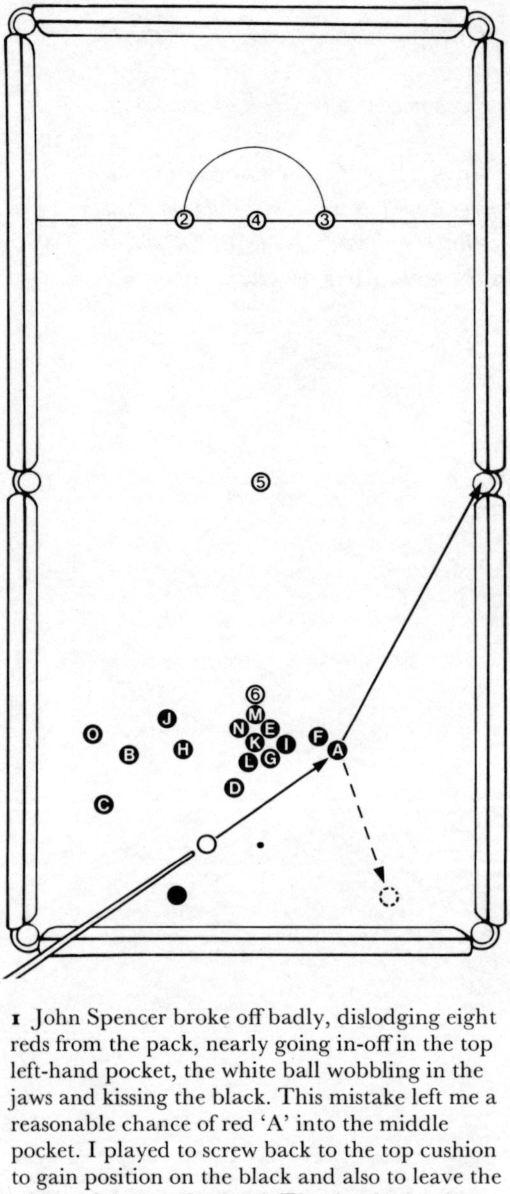

1 John Spencer broke off badly, dislodging eight reds from the pack, nearly going in-off in the top left-hand pocket, the white ball wobbling in the jaws and kissing the black. This mistake left me a reasonable chance of red 'A' into the middle pocket. I played to screw back to the top cushion to gain position on the black and also to leave the white safe in case I missed. The shot had to be struck quite firmly to obtain the screw-back I required. This made the pot slightly harder. The red rattled a bit in the jaws, but dropped in. At the same time, the white ball screwed back to the top cushion just as I planned. 1 point.

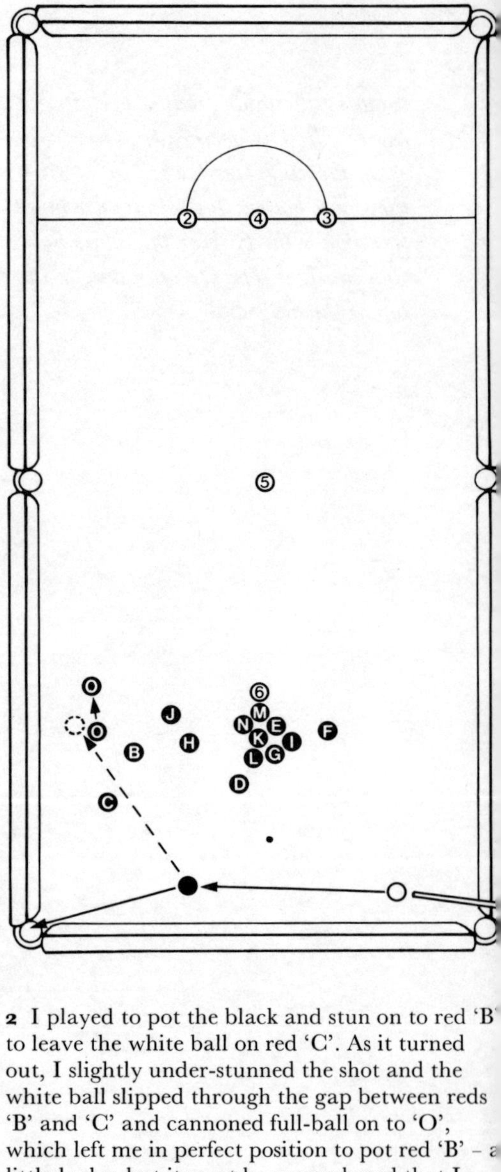

2 I played to pot the black and stun on to red 'B' to leave the white ball on red 'C'. As it turned out, I slightly under-stunned the shot and the white ball slipped through the gap between reds 'B' and 'C' and cannoned full-ball on to 'O', which left me in perfect position to pot red 'B' – a little lucky, but it must be remembered that I was still struggling to get into the game and I had yet to cue well in the match. 8 points.

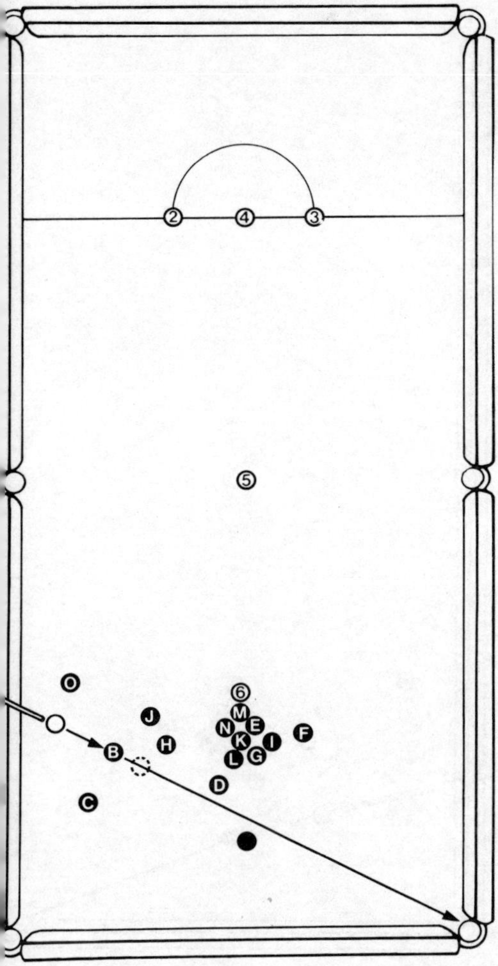

This was a simple stun shot to leave the white all in roughly the same position as red 'B', with nice angle on the black. 9 points.

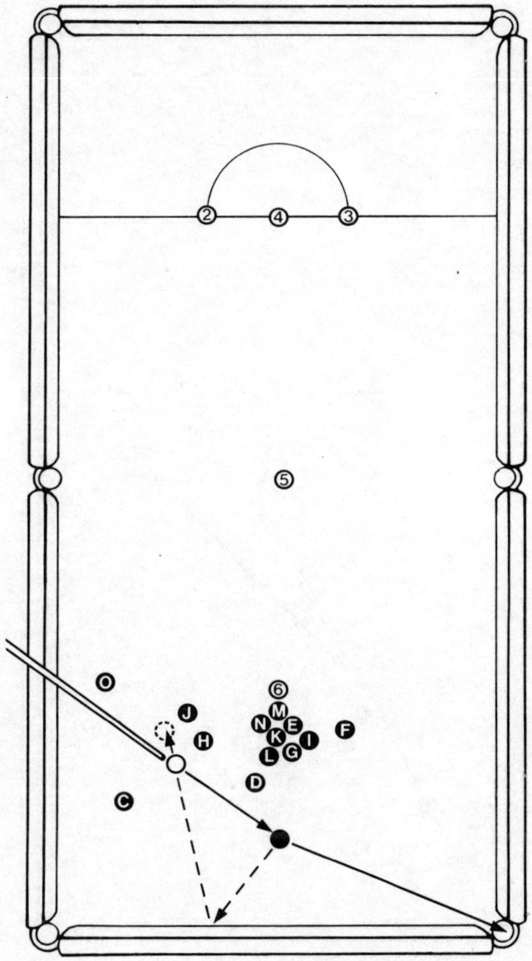

4 I decided red 'D' would be the ideal ball to take next as it would open up more reds into potable positions. I stunned the black in to try to bring the white ball back roughly into its original position. At the back of my mind I knew that I didn't have to be spot on because I would always be well-placed for red 'C', so I was not bothered when I played the shot a little too hard. 16 points.

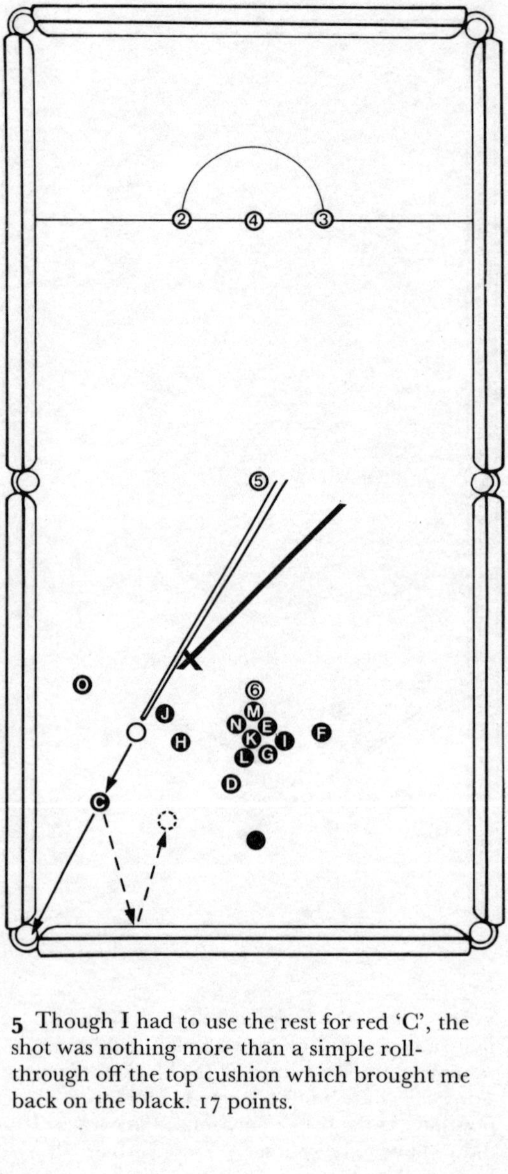

5 Though I had to use the rest for red 'C', the shot was nothing more than a simple roll-through off the top cushion which brought me back on the black. 17 points.

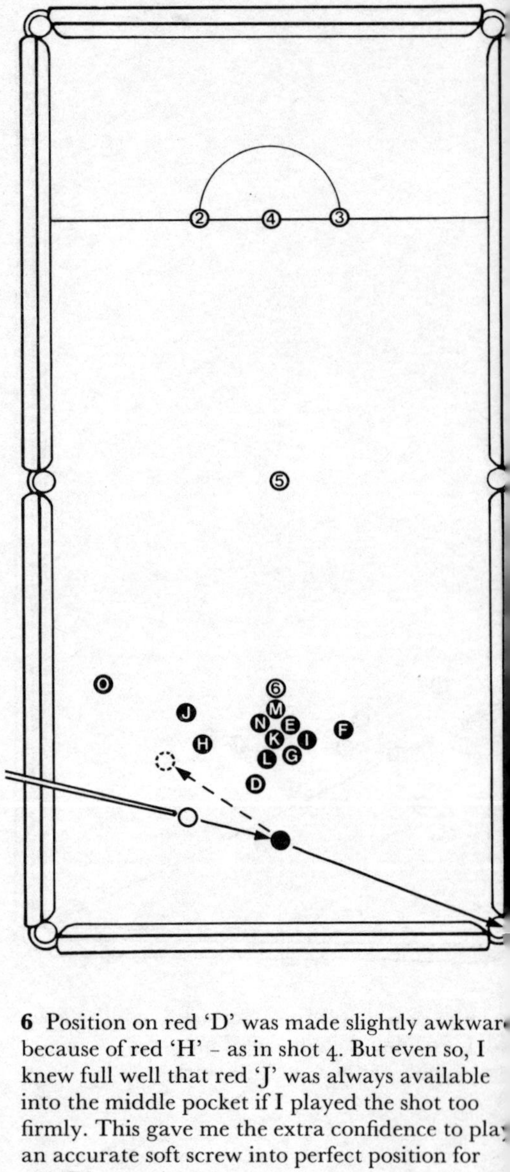

6 Position on red 'D' was made slightly awkwar because of red 'H' – as in shot 4. But even so, I knew full well that red 'J' was always available into the middle pocket if I played the shot too firmly. This gave me the extra confidence to pla an accurate soft screw into perfect position for red 'D'. 24 points.

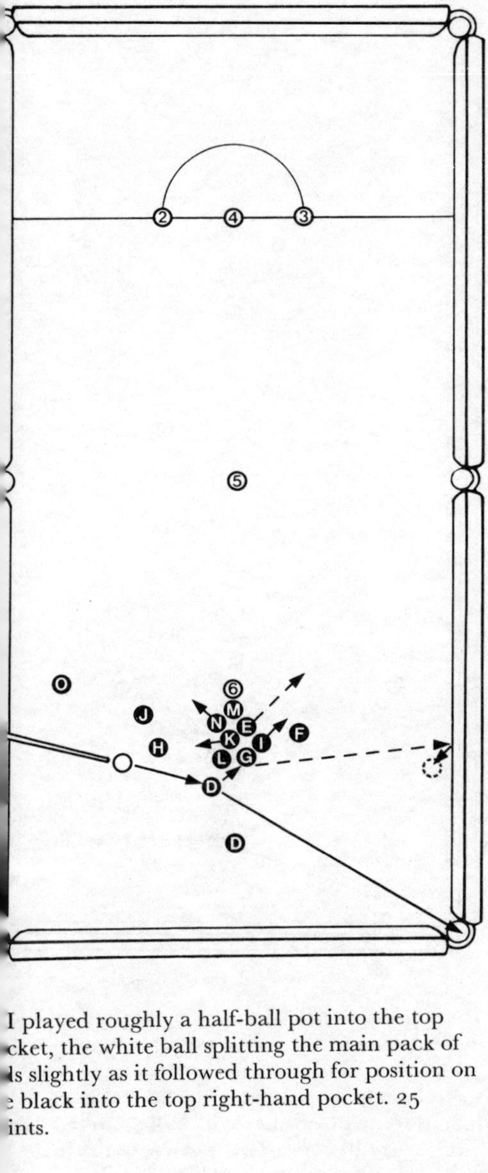

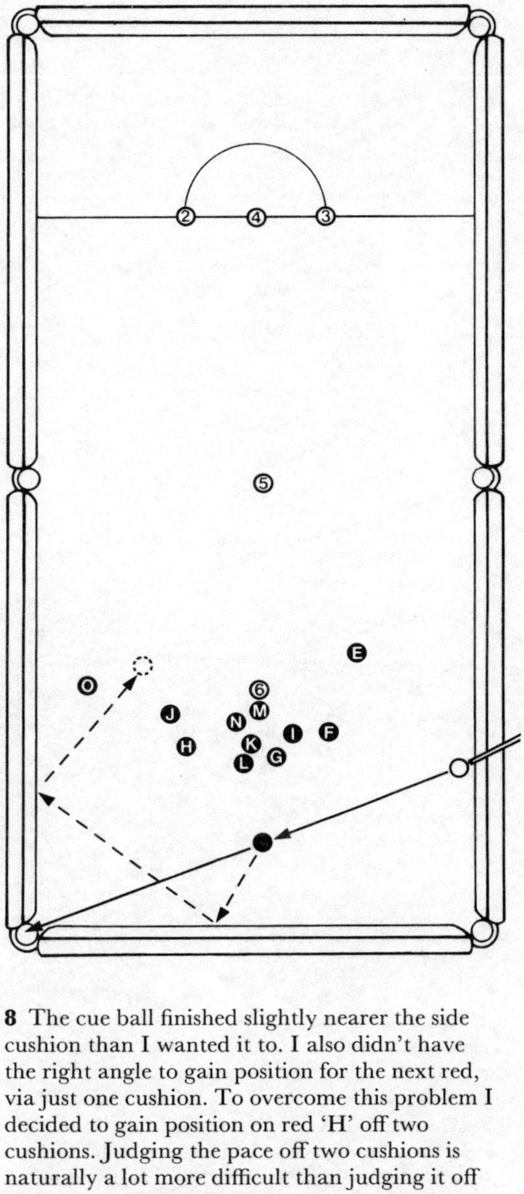

I played roughly a half-ball pot into the top
cket, the white ball splitting the main pack of
ls slightly as it followed through for position on
e black into the top right-hand pocket. 25
ints.

8 The cue ball finished slightly nearer the side cushion than I wanted it to. I also didn't have the right angle to gain position for the next red, via just one cushion. To overcome this problem I decided to gain position on red 'H' off two cushions. Judging the pace off two cushions is naturally a lot more difficult than judging it off one, and I rolled through fractionally farther than I planned, as can be seen from the dotted white ball, and left myself no obvious red to pot. 32 points.

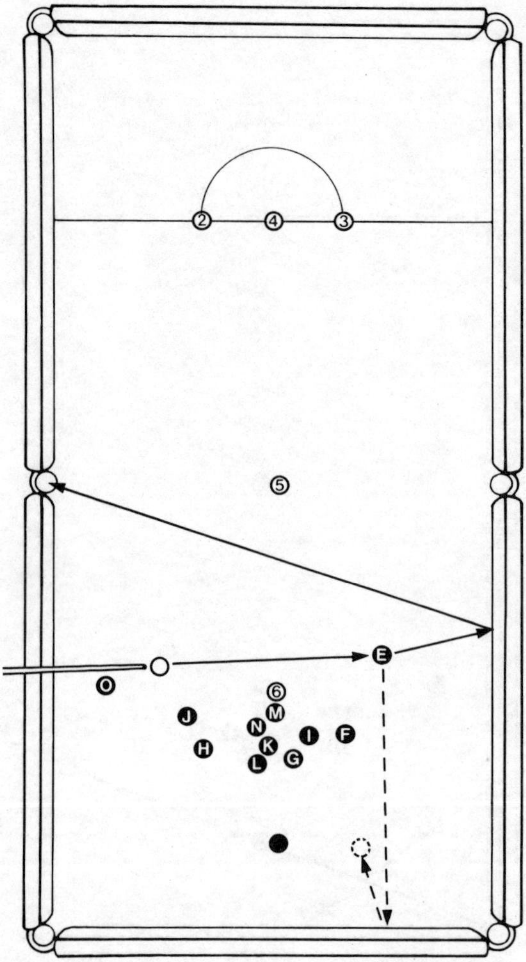

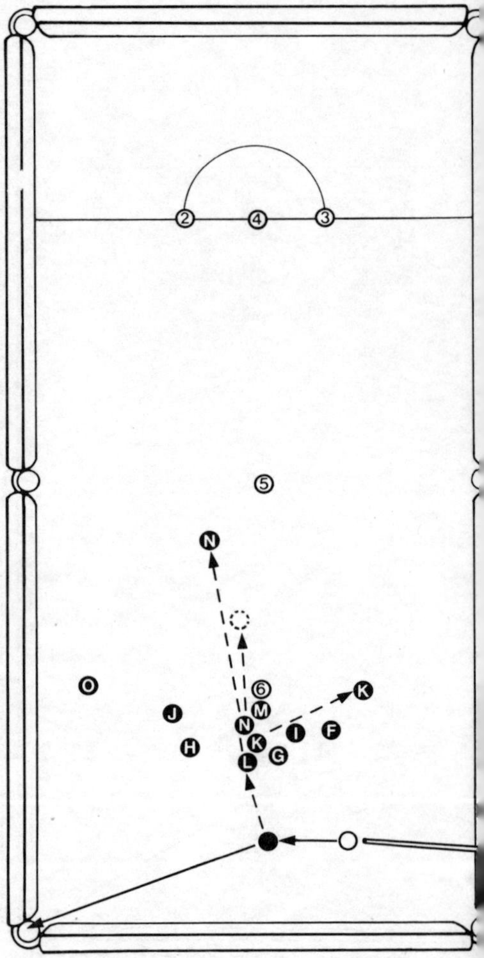

9 Later on, while watching the frame on video, I heard commentator John Pulman also say that he couldn't see an obvious red and, in fact, predicted that I would play a safety shot, sending the white ball down the table. But I could see a fairly easy double (red 'E') with a reasonable chance of safety if I missed. This meant having to screw the white ball past the pack to the top cushion to leave it on the black. Even though doubles are never certainties, I was very confident about this particular one. It never touched the sides. 33 points.

10 This was a critical shot, as a player can neve guarantee, when screwing the white ball into th pack, where the balls will end up – the white sometimes burying itself in the pack. I knew I had to try to direct the white ball on to red 'L', but it was still not certain to come out in my favour. Rather surprisingly, only two reds actually moved after the white ball entered the pack. Both came to rest in easy, potable positio – away from a cushion – and, as a bonus, the white ball cleared itself from the pack, to end u unhampered by any reds and perfectly on 'F'. A element of luck is obviously needed to accompli a 147 break. 40 points.

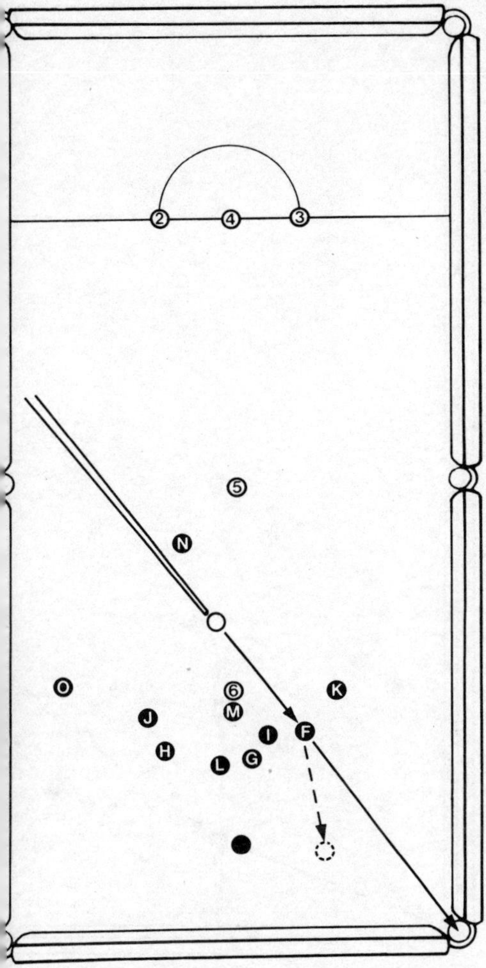

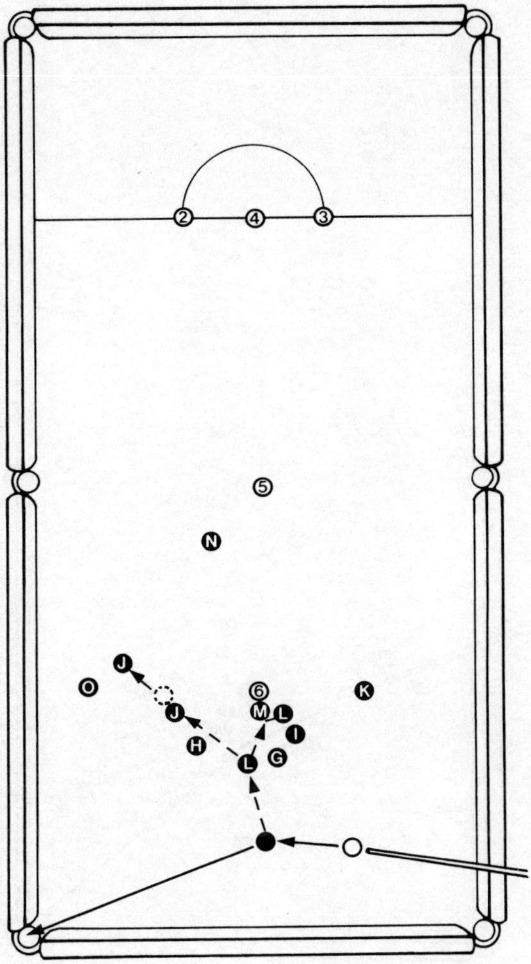

Red 'F' was an easy follow-through shot to in position on the black, which I snapped up. points.

12 It would have been silly to disturb the reds just for the sake of it, but I felt that stunning on to red 'L' was the correct ploy as it would open up more possibilities for position on the black. Though winning the frame was more important to me than taking undue risks to record a 147, I had decided, with the position of the balls, that the opportunity was too good to miss. David Taylor, working as a commentator, thought the same, although John Pulman, a more experienced commentator, thought it was a little early to talk about a potential maximum. 48 points.

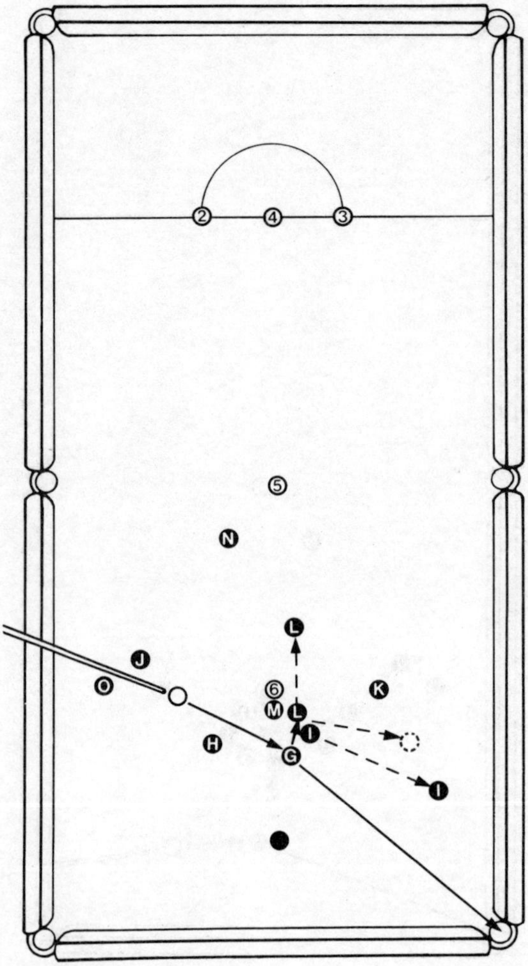

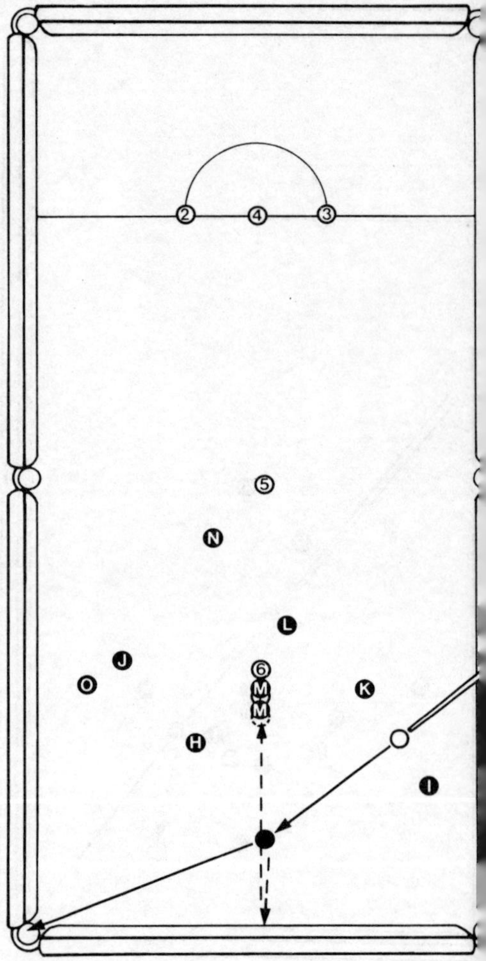

13 All of a sudden I had a problem. I was slightly the wrong side of 'G' to pot it and be able to run through for the black without disturbing another red. Instead, I knew the white ball would cannon into both 'L' and 'I', splitting them, and would then roll through for a position on the black. What worried me was the chance, as often happens, that I would end up snookering myself on red 'I'. I also had to use more top-spin on the white to counteract the slowing effect it would suffer when cannoning into the reds. Even so, I decided too much 'top' would leave me snookered by 'I', so I played the shot firmly enough to get the white ball moving forward but, hopefully, without too much spin to catch up 'I'. As you can see from the path of the white ball, if 'I' had been a little slower, or the white ball slightly faster, I would have ended up snookered. As it was, I obtained perfect position on the black. 49 points.

14 This was an easy black, as there were few places on the table where I could fail to find a red to get back on the black. I knew the natura route of the white ball would take it towards th pink and red 'M'. With this in mind, I played t drop on to 'M', hopefully splitting it from the pink and leaving the white ball on red 'H'. 56 points.

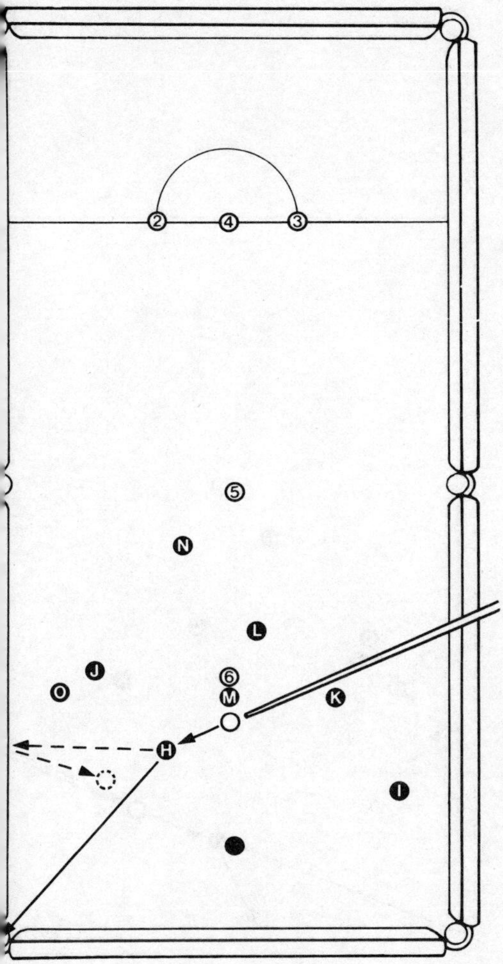

. The shot on red 'H' was not a natural follow-rough, as the white ball needed a little bit of t-hand 'side' to keep it comfortably near the ack. 57 points.

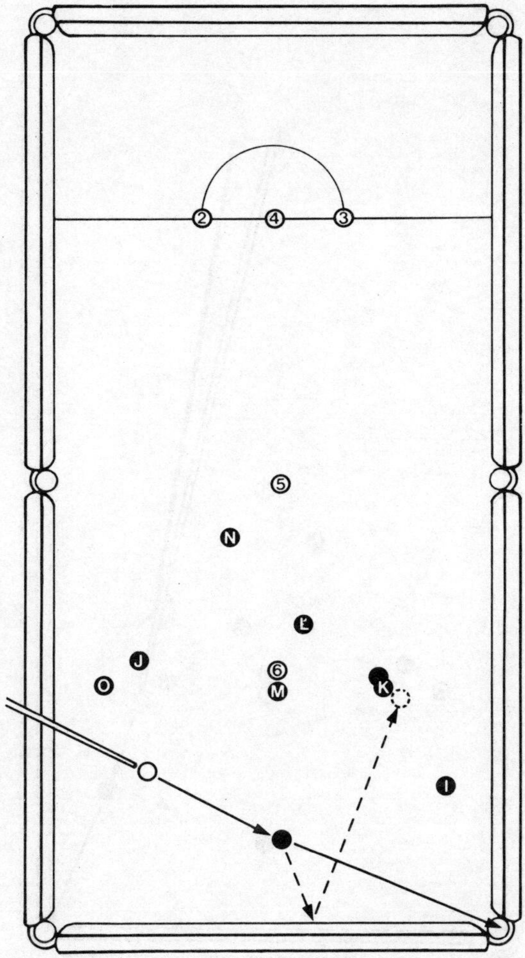

16 While preparing to pot the black, I could see I was again left with a choice of reds for my next shot because they were nicely split apart. In sinking the black, I tried to send the white ball into the area just past red 'K', knowing that a full-ball kiss on red 'K' would leave me on red 'I'. What happened could have proved serious. I hit the shot a little below strength, and the white ball threatened to end up so close to red 'K' that I would be pressed into using the spider to try to pot red 'I'. Fortunately for me the white ball just went to the right of 'K', leaving me a clean shot at 'I'. 64 points.

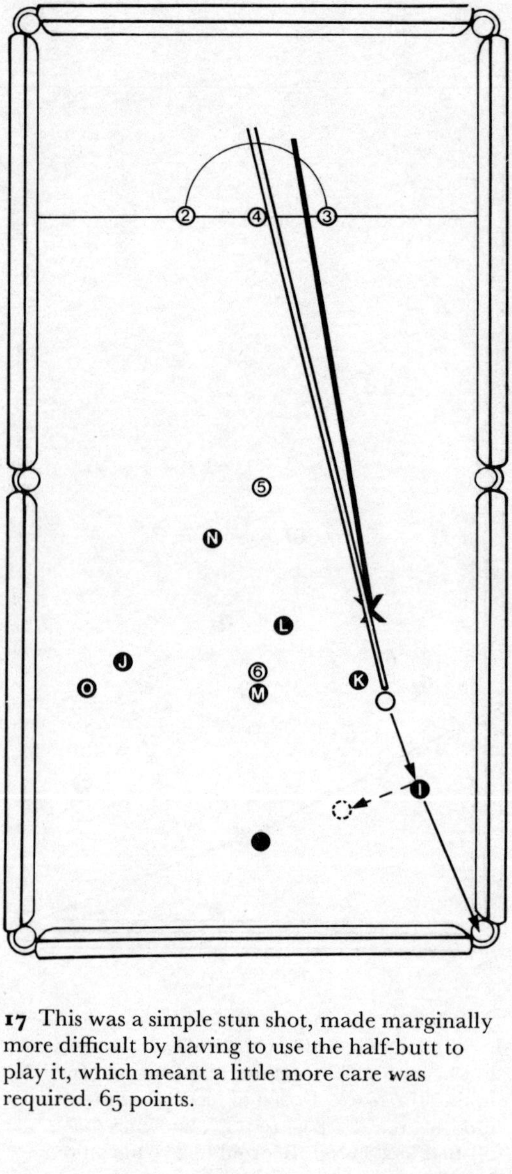

17 This was a simple stun shot, made marginally more difficult by having to use the half-butt to play it, which meant a little more care was required. 65 points.

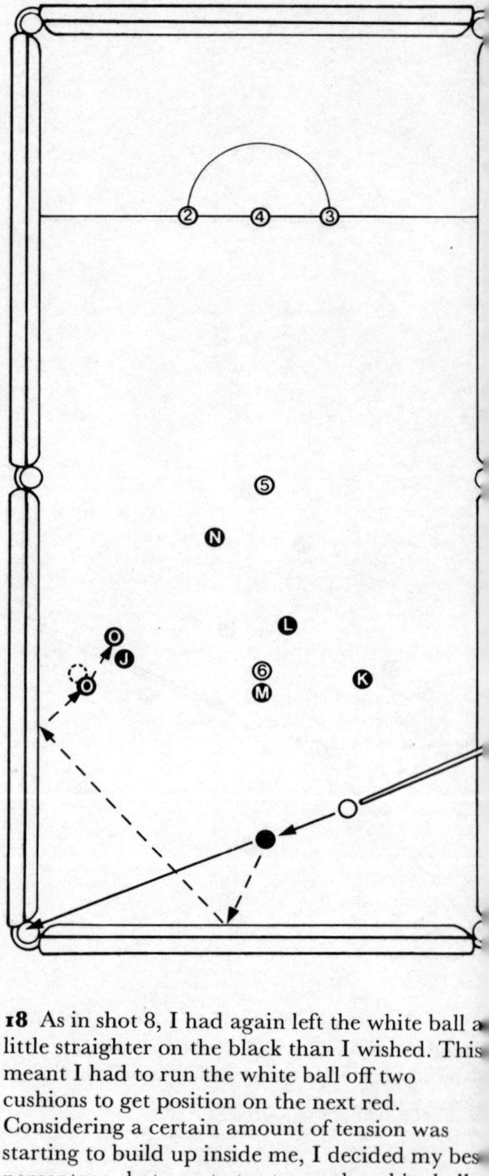

18 As in shot 8, I had again left the white ball a little straighter on the black than I wished. This meant I had to run the white ball off two cushions to get position on the next red. Considering a certain amount of tension was starting to build up inside me, I decided my bes percentage shot was to try to get the white ball around the back of red 'O' to leave the white ba on that red, or 'J' or 'M', with a view to potting one of them into a top pocket. In potting the black I cannoned into red 'O' and left the white ball perfectly on 'J' for a pot into the middle pocket to get back on the black. Some people might have regarded this as lucky, but I would have been terribly unlucky if I had not ended u with some sort of position on at least one red, considering how well they were spread out. 72 points.

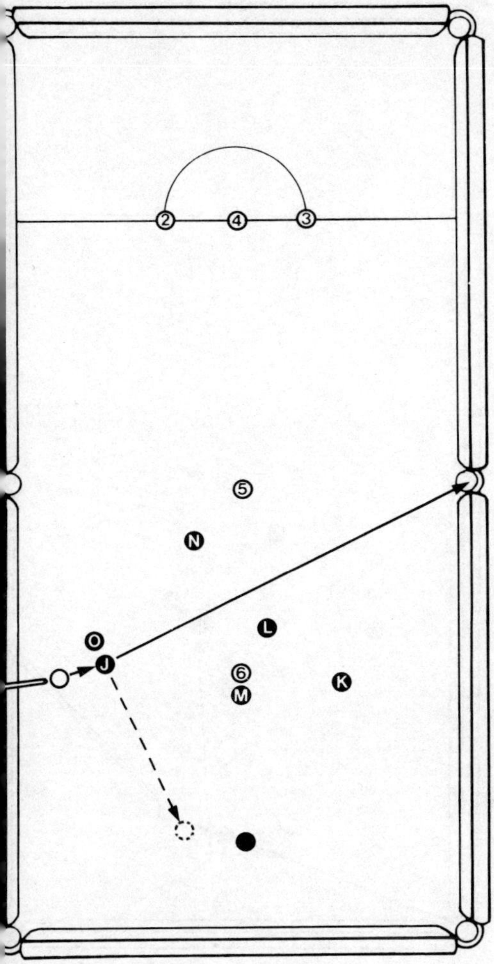

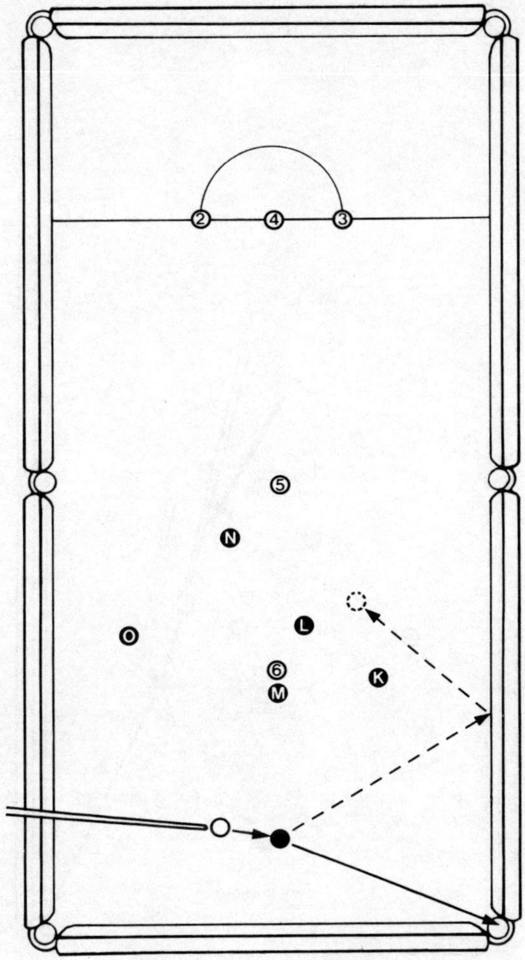

19 This just required a soft screw, sending the white slowly up the table towards the black. 73 points.

20 This was one shot that could not go wrong provided I hit the white ball hard enough to achieve position on 'K' into the top right-hand pocket. Anything harder would have left me straightforward shots on 'L', 'M', 'N' and even 'K' into the top left-hand pocket. 80 points.

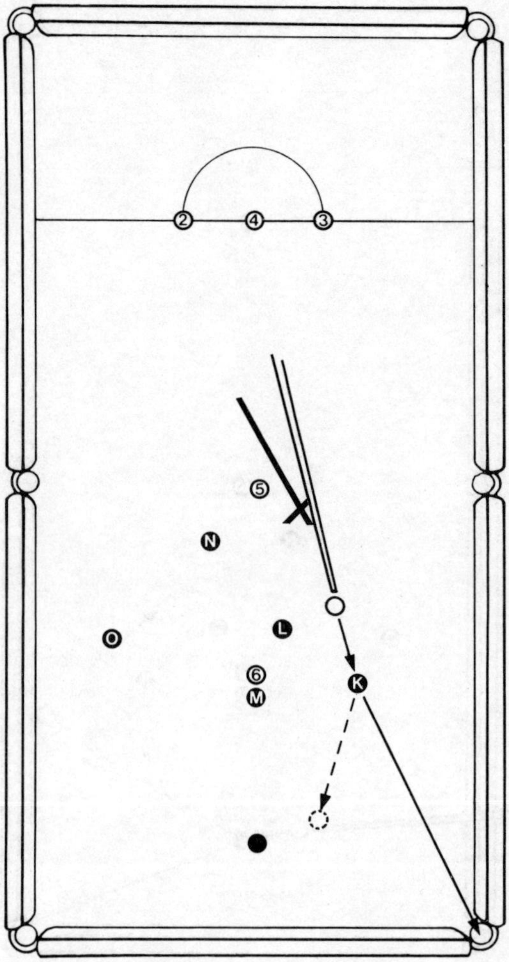

21 I ended up taking red 'K' into the top left-hand pocket. By now the tension was gripping everyone, and even the least observant had worked out that a 147 was on. Every shot was receiving increased attention, from the crowd and from me. There was a real air of expectation in the hall. Everyone was on my side – even John! Though red 'K' was not a particularly difficult pot, a slight problem arose because I had to send the white ball dangerously close to the black. I had the choice of trundling the white ball gently through, or playing it off the top cushion, round the back of the black, to pot it into the same pocket as the red. Though not apparent to most people, this really was a mini crisis. I chose to play the softer shot, which was liable to lack confidence, especially as tension affects the strength of shots as well as accuracy, but more likely to leave me good position. I judged the weight of the shot perfectly, and David Taylor complimented me on it. 81 points.

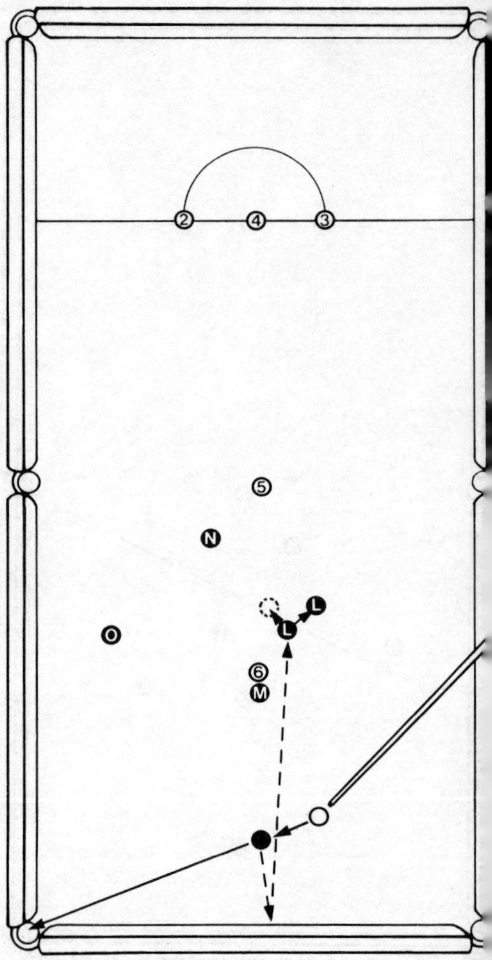

22 In potting the black, I now decided to try t play position on red 'M' by bouncing off the to cushion and dropping on to red 'L'. 88 points.

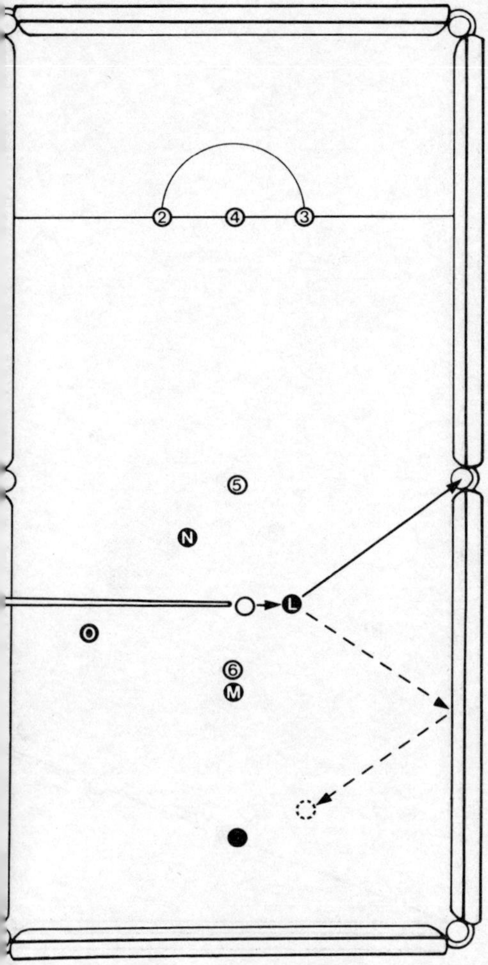

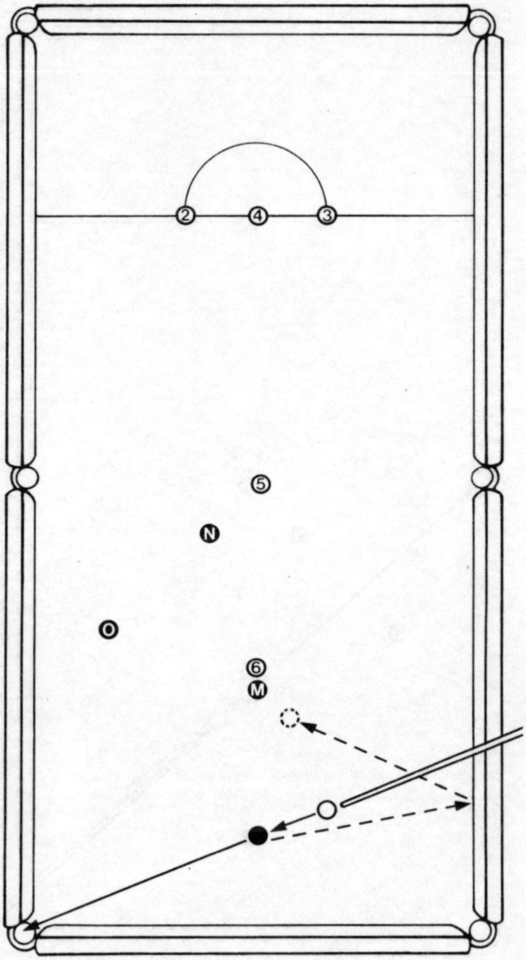

I was not far out, but far enough, the white
ll clipping 'L' on the wrong side. The other
e would have kept me on 'M'. Even so I could
w roll 'L' into the middle pocket and still get
ck on to the black, which I did. 89 points.

24 I probably came to rest in the worst possible place for gaining position on another red. I was just off dead straight and on the wrong side of the black to screw back up the table. Also, I was so straight that if I tried to run the white through off the top and side cushions, I would almost certainly strike the jaws of the top pocket. Looking around the table, I could see 'M' was potable into the middle pocket, so I had to decide whether to screw back a couple of feet or play the slightly more difficult shot of screwing back off the side cushion to get in line with 'M'. Playing this shot would make the pot, and the shot back on to the black, much easier to control. I played it to perfection. 96 points.

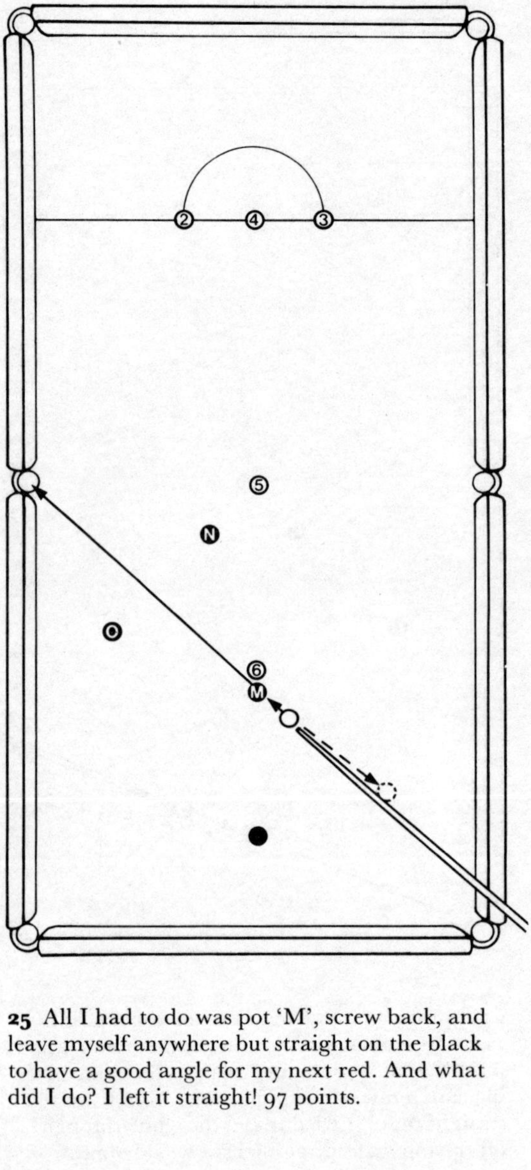

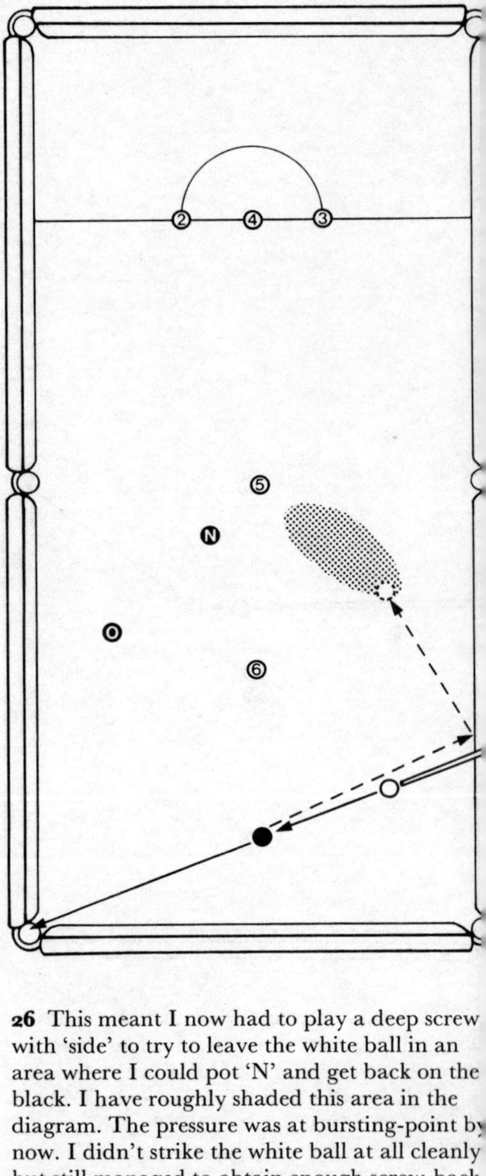

25 All I had to do was pot 'M', screw back, and leave myself anywhere but straight on the black to have a good angle for my next red. And what did I do? I left it straight! 97 points.

26 This meant I now had to play a deep screw with 'side' to try to leave the white ball in an area where I could pot 'N' and get back on the black. I have roughly shaded this area in the diagram. The pressure was at bursting-point by now. I didn't strike the white ball at all cleanly but still managed to obtain enough screw-back and 'side' to bring it dead in line with 'M'. Anything short of this would have been fatal, a would have had to send the white ball into bau to return to the black. 104 points.

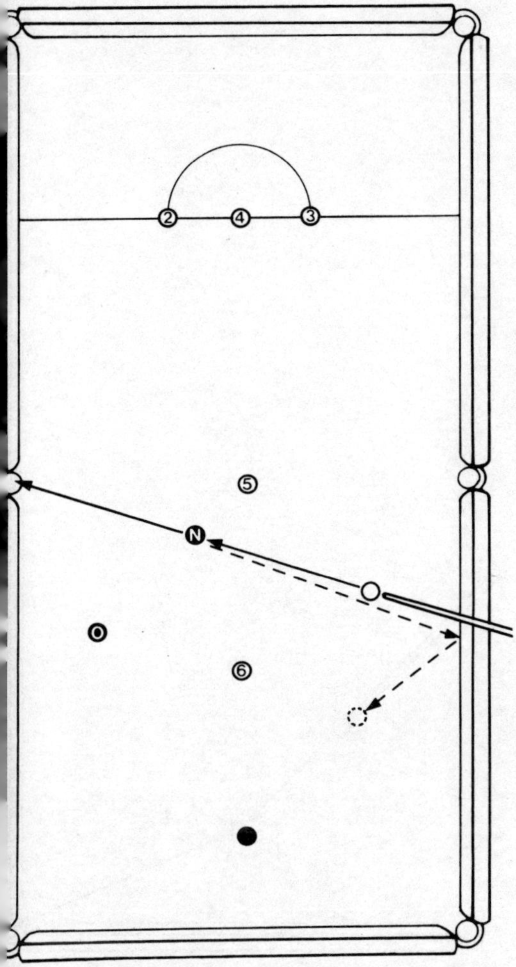

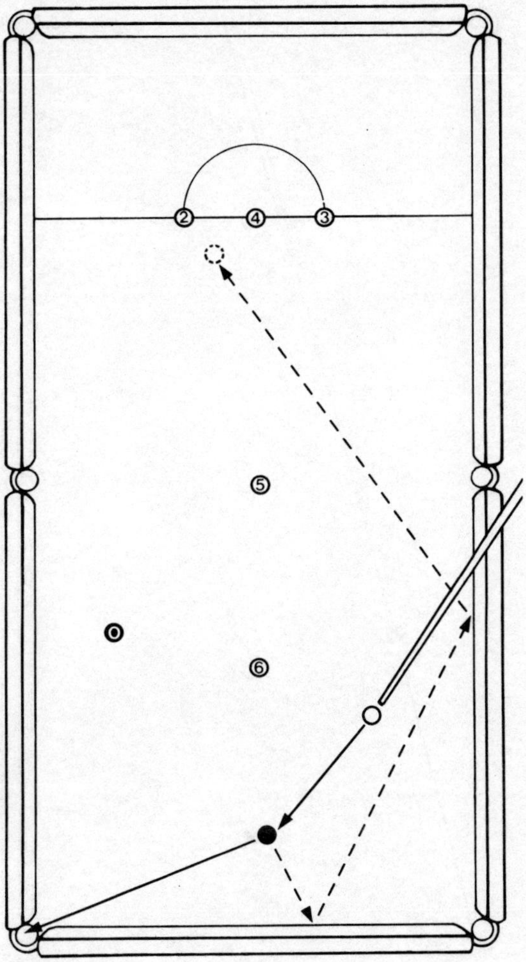

7 Even so, I had created a problem for myself
: I now had to play an even deeper screw-back
ith right-hand 'side' to have any hope of
turning to the black. I potted red 'N' and
rewed back well, slightly out of position, but
eping my chances alive. 105 points.

28 I was neither near enough, nor had the right angle, to gain position on the next red and, at the same time, confidently play the black. At first the only way I could see open to me was to try a delicate slow cut with a lot of right-hand 'side' but, considering the pressure on me, I was sure I would miss. In view of this, I chose to stun the black into the top corner pocket, sending the white ball off the top and side cushions and down past the blue to give myself a fighting chance of a long, straight pot, one of my favourites, which I knew I could get provided I could keep myself together. The only risk in playing such a shot was that I might leave myself hampered by the yellow or brown. The black disappeared and I waited for the white ball to come to a stop. 112 points.

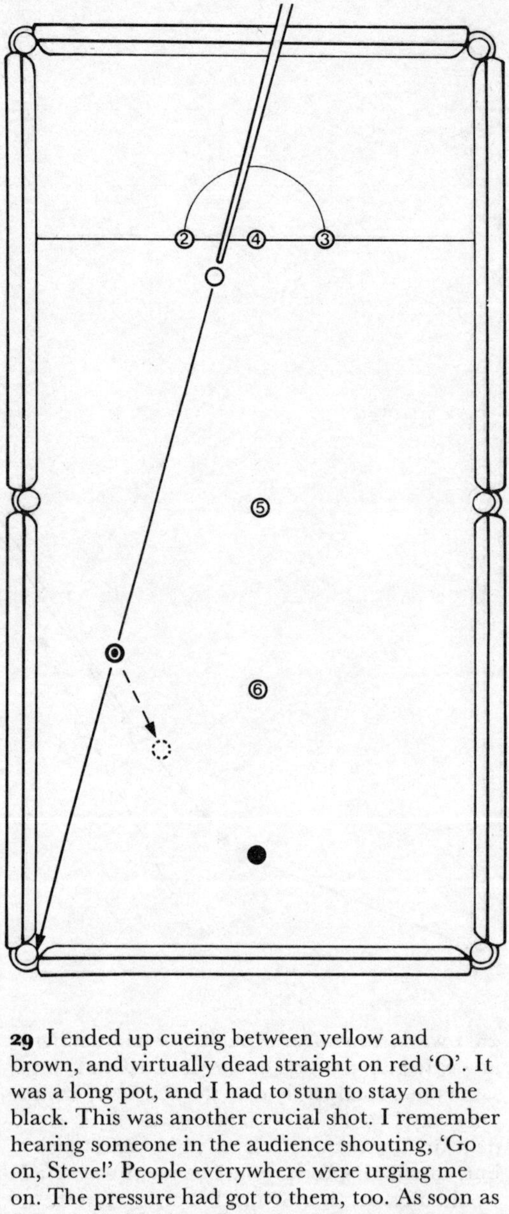

29 I ended up cueing between yellow and brown, and virtually dead straight on red 'O'. It was a long pot, and I had to stun to stay on the black. This was another crucial shot. I remember hearing someone in the audience shouting, 'Go on, Steve!' People everywhere were urging me on. The pressure had got to them, too. As soon as the red crashed into the hole, the crowd burst into life with obvious relief. I was so pleased I felt like clapping, myself. Looking back now, I realise it was the type of shot I could have been excused for missing. But I played it with so much confidence it flew into the pocket. 113 points.

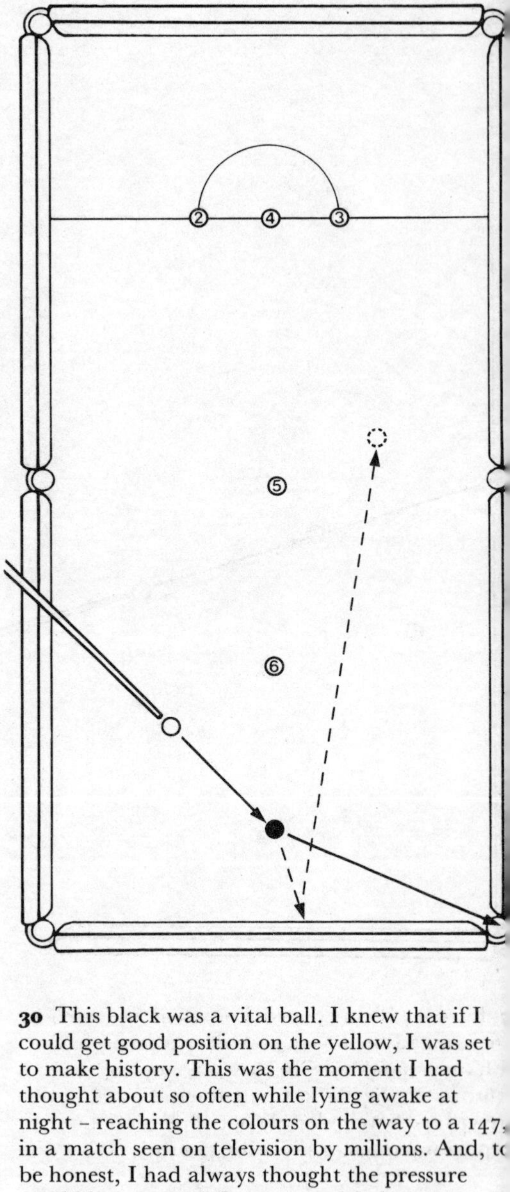

30 This black was a vital ball. I knew that if I could get good position on the yellow, I was set to make history. This was the moment I had thought about so often while lying awake at night – reaching the colours on the way to a 147, in a match seen on television by millions. And, to be honest, I had always thought the pressure would be too much for anyone. My heart was definitely beating faster. My pulse was racing. It was so different from the pressure I remembered in the world championships. This was just me against the table. There was no opponent to worry about. I told myself that, even though this was a fantastic chance to achieve the impossible dream, I must keep myself together and not panic. I potted the black with a little left-hand 'side' to avoid cannoning into the pink, and sent the white ball rolling down the table. 120 points.

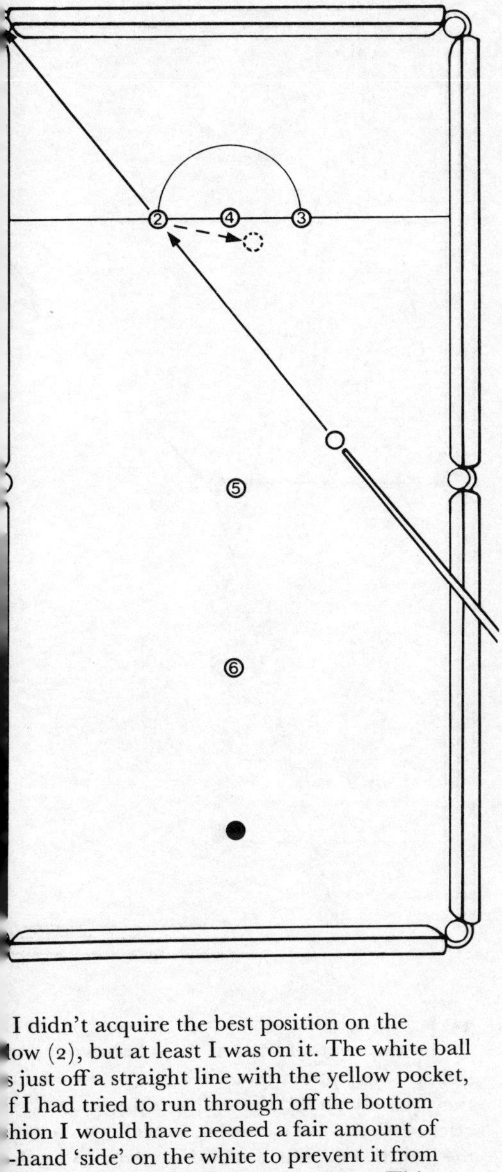

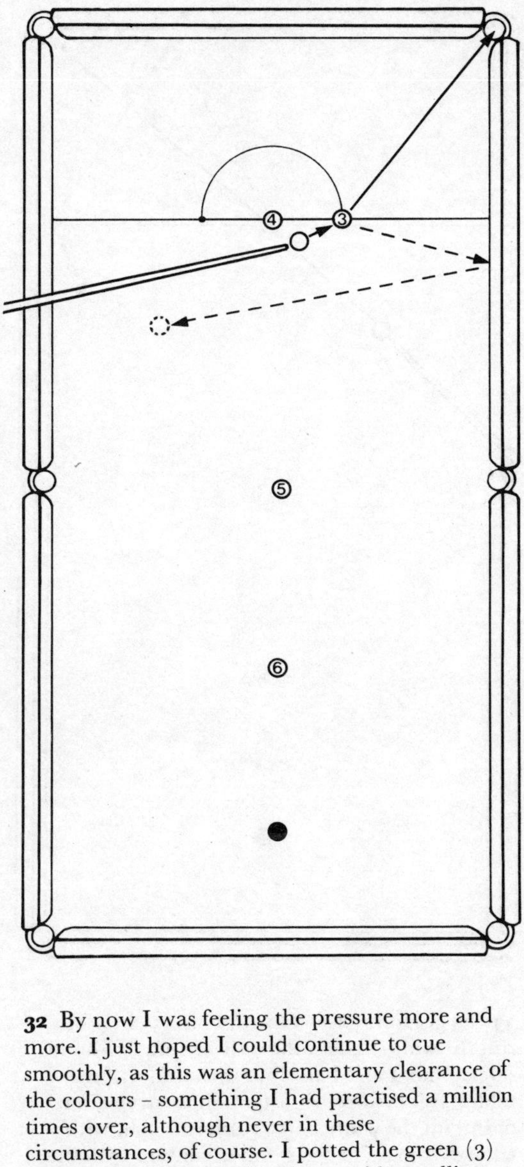

I didn't acquire the best position on the low (2), but at least I was on it. The white ball s just off a straight line with the yellow pocket, f I had tried to run through off the bottom hion I would have needed a fair amount of -hand 'side' on the white to prevent it from ling up near the bottom side cushion. This s a difficult shot regardless of pressure. My ernative was to screw back sharply, taking e to avoid the brown and snookering myself, often happens if you don't hit the shot crisply ough. I decided to approach the yellow this y, especially as it didn't need any of the eaded 'side'. I applied just enough screw-back the white ball to avoid hitting the brown and myself nicely placed on the green. 122 points.

32 By now I was feeling the pressure more and more. I just hoped I could continue to cue smoothly, as this was an elementary clearance of the colours – something I had practised a million times over, although never in these circumstances, of course. I potted the green (3) with a little left-hand 'side' to avoid travelling too far up the table. 125 points.

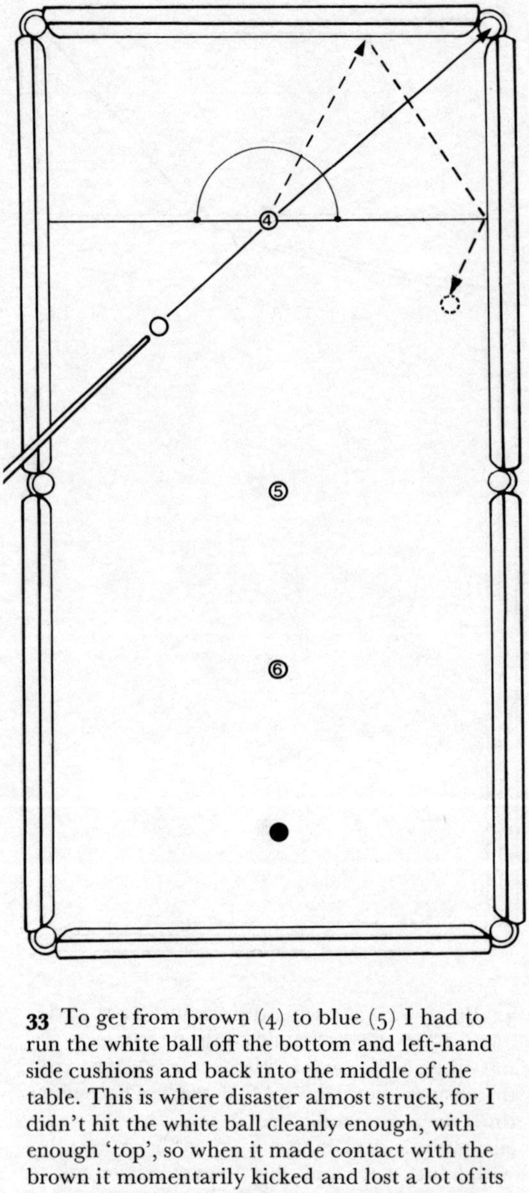

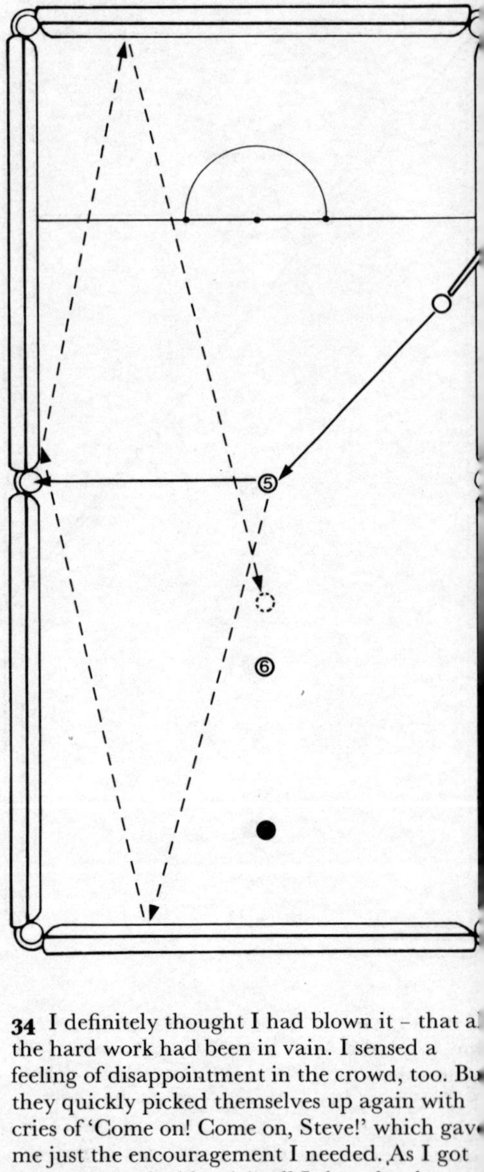

33 To get from brown (4) to blue (5) I had to run the white ball off the bottom and left-hand side cushions and back into the middle of the table. This is where disaster almost struck, for I didn't hit the white ball cleanly enough, with enough 'top', so when it made contact with the brown it momentarily kicked and lost a lot of its forward momentum. This meant it barely passed the baulk line and left me perilously close to the cushion and terribly placed on the blue. 129 points.

34 I definitely thought I had blown it – that a the hard work had been in vain. I sensed a feeling of disappointment in the crowd, too. Bu they quickly picked themselves up again with cries of 'Come on! Come on, Steve!' which gav me just the encouragement I needed. As I got down to pot the blue (5), all I thought about w getting the ball in the hole, and I hoped and prayed that the white would end up somewher favourably on the pink. My legs had turned to jelly by now. Meanwhile, up in the commenta box, David Taylor was saying that if anyone could pot the blue, 'This man can'. Ironically, the words were leaving his lips, you could see n shaking my head. The blue went in sweetly all right and I just prayed that the white ball wou end up on the pink (6). Unfortunately it endec up dead in line with the pink, about a foot awa leaving me another terribly difficult shot. Of a the shots I played in the frame, I regarded this blue as my best. 134 points.

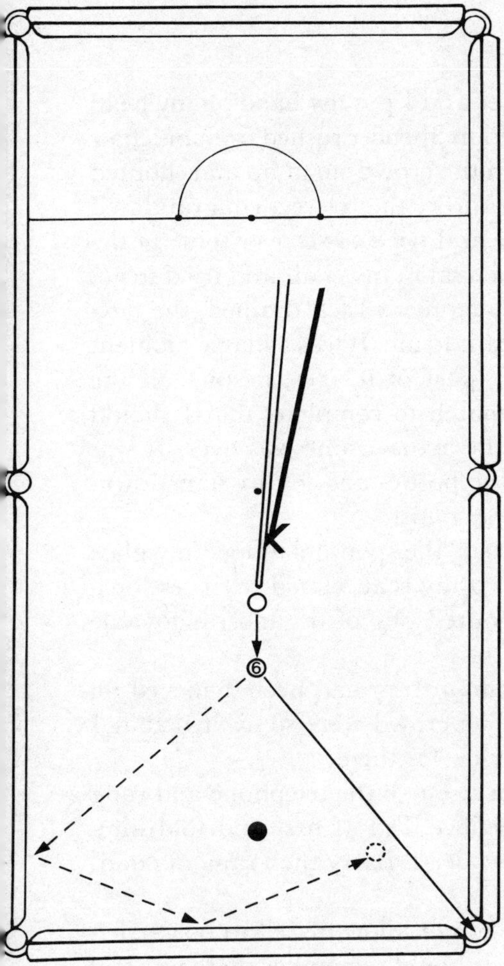

35 There are two ways of playing a shot like this one on the pink (6). You can cut the pink in with plenty of 'top', sending the white ball down the table into baulk and back again, hopefully ending up in a position to pot the black, or you can screw the white ball sharply on to the side cushion and around behind the black to gain position that way. Using the rest, I chose the sharp screw, played the shot to perfection, and the pink rocketed into the corner pocket. 140 points.

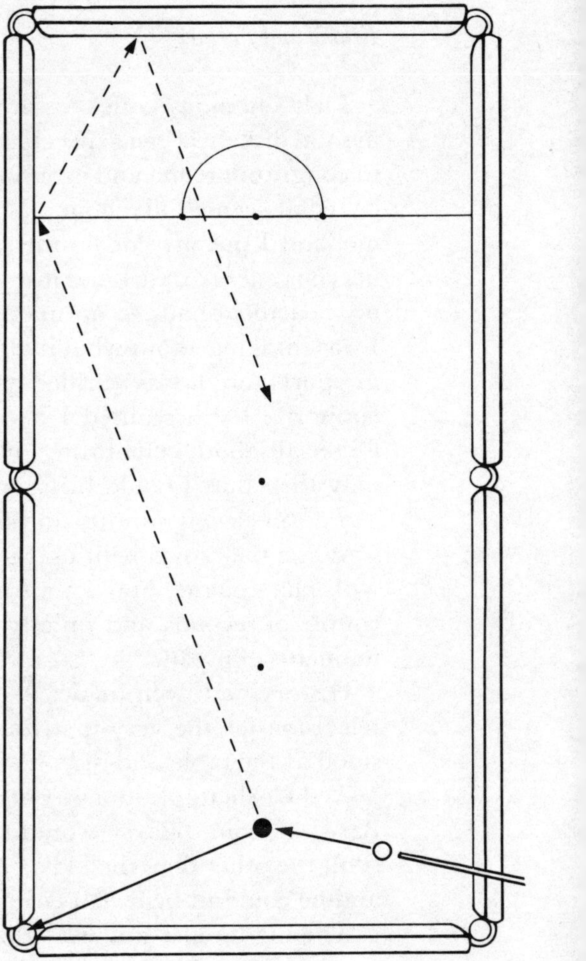

36 The crowd were going wild. I think most of them thought I wouldn't pot the pink because it looked more difficult than the blue. As soon as the pink went down, I was just one shot away from another historic moment. Lada, the sponsors, were offering a brand-new car to anyone who achieved the 147, but I thought of it only once during the break, when I was on 47. The actual car was no incentive; I was interested only in the honour and prestige of accomplishing Misson Impossible. Having potted the pink, I very slowly put the rest away, trying hard to compose myself for the vital last shot. I walked around the table, stood behind the black and felt confident of potting it. The only danger I could think of now was going in-off. I was definitely not as nervous then as I was on the blue. As the black rolled in I was still not satisfied that I was over the line. I followed the white ball down the table with my eyes until I was sure it wasn't heading in-off. And then I realised I had made it. I had achieved a whole frame of snooker perfection.

I felt a nervous smile cross my face and I put my hand on my head in total disbelief. I was speechless. John Spencer rushed from his chair to congratulate me and everyone in the crowd stood up and shouted for what seemed like hours. Jim Thorpe, the referee, congratulated me, and I put my cue on the table and tried to recover some of the nervous energy that I had lost. I then sat in my chair and tried to get my heartbeat back to normal. One moment I felt drained, the next I was thinking about what it all meant to me. It was a magic moment in sport and I was thrilled to be part of it. Yet, despite all the euphoria, I still realised I had a match to complete, that I should forget all about celebrating until the actual game was over. It was only then that I could bring out the bottles and let my hair down. 147 . . . in eleven minutes and nine seconds!

While the crowd kept up their roar, the sponsors topped my glass with champagne, and I returned to my seat, closed my eyes for a couple of seconds and quietly savoured one of the most enjoyable moments of my life.

History had been made. A maximum 147 had been achieved on television for the very first time. The crowd were so excited that I stood at the table and did an interview for them.

Ted Corbett, of the *Daily Star*, beat me to the telephone and rang Barry at home. Barry wouldn't believe Ted at first and told him, 'Pull the other one, the kid's on his knees!' Barry then rang my dad, and he couldn't believe it either.

The big danger now was that I might allow myself to be carried away by it all. It was essential that I should remember there was still a tournament to be won. I couldn't go on dreaming about one frame for the rest of my life.

As the crowd finally cooled down, I stood up to start frame six, and I told myself that I had to concentrate hard, and forget everything that had gone on before. I managed to win that frame, which put me 4–2 in front, and then I took the next one as well, to win the match 5–2.

When I made my first mistake after the 147, I remember Spencer saying 'rubbish' out aloud, which I found quite funny. John has always been one of the best wind-up merchants in the business.

Later on that evening I watched a recording of the 147 on television and I felt a lump come to my throat when it was all over. I fancied a lie-in next morning, but I had to be out at eleven for a photographic session, and in the evening I was due to play Ray Reardon in the semi-final.

I was so exhausted before going out to play Reardon that I fell asleep in the Pressroom. My human clock was still not functioning properly. I couldn't shake off the jet-lag. I kept waking up at ridiculous hours. It was only when I started playing at the table that I really became conscious. The rest of the time I went round in a daze.

Considering I felt so dozy, it was hardly surprising that I couldn't settle into any rhythm, though I did hear the alarm bells ringing when things look grim against Reardon. I woke just in time to produce something special with a century break in the last frame to nick the match 6–5.

This victory put me in the final against Terry Griffiths. Who else? But again I was only slightly better than semi-conscious. I trailed 4–3 at the interval and fell soundly asleep in the Pressroom. I drew a chair to the table, put my head on my arms and went dead for an hour. Then I revived, took a shower, and dressed for the evening session.

Back at the table, I still felt rotten, and this showed in just about every shot I played until I eventually managed to pull myself together into some sort of shape. Unfortunately for me, in the time I was regaining consciousness, Terry was building a commanding 8–3 lead and needed only one more frame to take the match.

At this point I told myself I must try harder. I had to start taking more risks. And with this in mind, I drew on reserves I never thought were in me. I clawed my way back to 8–8 and set up the most thrilling finish I can remember in any major tournament.

By now I was firing on all cylinders. The adrenalin was rushing around and Terry was in a visible sweat. Not even Hitchcock could have imagined a more dramatic climax. The pink and black would win me the match.

The pink was an extremely difficult long shot, with the cue-ball tucked tight under the bottom cushion, making it terribly hard for me to strike the white with any real force. Despite this problem I thought it would be more difficult to play safe than to go for the pot. If I missed the pot, I was fairly confident the white would run to safety anyway. At the same time, I decided that if I potted the pink, I would go flat out for the black, no matter where I finished up. The black itself was just off the side-cushion, halfway down the table.

I potted the pink and felt very pleased with myself. The crowd were getting more and more on my side as the fightback continued. I think there were as many who wanted me to win as wanted Terry to win, because of the tremendous change in fortunes.

After potting the pink, I smiled quietly to myself. At times it is advisable to have the first crack at the black, because the second chance may never come. I knew that if I missed the pot, the white ball was certain to stay on the cushion and cause Terry a problem when he came to cue.

I drove hard at the black, and for a split second it seemed I had pulled off a miraculous win, but the ball rattled in the jaws and decided to stay out. Meanwhile the white didn't come to rest as close to the cushion as I had hoped, and Terry was able to make good contact with the cue-ball, which was placed virtually behind the black and in a direct line to the corner pocket.

As the black went down for the last time, Terry staggered to his chair, one hand on the table, the other on his head, making it clear to everyone that he was glad the battle was over. It was like climbing Everest eight times on the same day, he said later when interviewed on television.

I have looked at my attempt to pot that black several times on video and I've thought deeply about it. Given the same circumstances again, I would approach the shot in exactly the same way. Everything was going well for me at the time, and there was no point in suddenly playing safe and becoming all defensive. Even though I missed the shot, I was satisfied with it. But it could have come out a little better for me in the end.

Civic appreciation for the 147 came from the Mayor of Oldham. He presented me with a plaque and said that only two other people had been honoured there in this way before.

13
The Master at the Masters

Discussions began immediately on whether I should do a voice-over of the 147 in a special half-hour programme for Granada, the company who televised the tournament in the first place. Having been guaranteed a satisfactory percentage for ourselves, and for the World Professional Billiards and Snooker Association, Barry and I agreed that such a programme could go ahead.

In a further bid to take advantage of their sponsorship, Lada put together a mock-up version of the number-plate SD 147, attached it to one of their cars, and took a photograph of me standing next to it. Several newspapers used the photograph, and Lada explained that they had failed to obtain the real number-plate in time for the picture.

Three weeks later, a Scots chap rang Barry and said he had something we wanted. It was a Datsun car, with the registration SD 147. The car was worth £2,000, but the Scotsman wanted £10,000. Barry told him to take a running jump off Ben Nevis.

He came back again a week later, saying his price had dropped to £6,000. Barry asked him to 'stop talking in silly figures', and stressed that £2,000 was our absolute maximum, but that he could keep the car.

As far as I'm concerned, personalised number-plates are a luxury, an ego trip. I have no intention of spending a fortune to have one. I am not that flash, anyway. All I do know is that this particular plate is not worth a penny to anyone else. Only a fool would turn down a sensible offer. Ironically, it is not so long since I kept seeing a car with the plates POT 147S, and I must admit that one or two pleasant thoughts crossed my mind at the time.

The enormous publicity that followed the 147 almost equalled the Press coverage I received when winning the world championships. Shortly after the Lada, I was invited to the annual *Daily Star* luncheon. Many showbusiness people were there, including Jimmy Tarbuck, Terry Wogan and Diana Dors. It seemed everyone had enjoyed the 147 on television and wanted to congratulate me. More than that, they showed a genuine interest in snooker and were eager to talk about it.

In the same way as most sportsmen admire the ability of people in showbusiness, most showbusiness people have a real appreciation of the skills of sportsmen. There is a definite mutual respect.

A highlight of the lunch was Jimmy Tarbuck constantly taking the micky out of Terry Wogan. Then, just as Terry was about to retaliate, a waitress dropped all the plates, and Bobby Moore's chair completely collapsed under him. He crashed to the floor and the place rocked with laughter. Terry's chance had gone for ever.

Business lunches seemed to rule my life at that time, but I could hardly complain when John Courage, the brewers, invited me to London to sign a contract that could earn me up to £300,000 over three years for making personal appearances on their behalf.

Courages were already well established as one of the country's biggest sponsors in sport, particularly through their close links with the England soccer squad. I had already appeared in a number of one-off promotions for the company, most of them expertly organised by Sue Roberts of Courage Central. I liked the way they worked, and I jumped at the chance of establishing a long-term exclusive contract with them. They guaranteed me £100,000 a year, but said that £20,000 would be deducted if I lost either the United Kingdom or the world championships. I saw the deal as another fine incentive for me to try hard.

Seriously though, the best thing about the Courage contract is that it keeps me in close touch with the average club member – the type of bloke who can't afford a ticket to the plushier places where I seem to spend most of my time these days.

Thanks to a good manager, and the popularity of snooker, I have become a bit too expensive for the normal club night. But now, through the Courage deal, I can enjoy the best of both worlds. On the one hand I have the smaller, appreciative audiences, and on the other I can earn the big money in the larger, less personal venues.

After all the publicity surrounding the Courage contract, money became the inevitable first question whenever I met anyone socially. Although it is a huge contract by any standard, money itself rarely crosses my mind. I enjoy playing snooker too much to think about cash and what it can buy. I just think about winning!

Money is mainly a game that Barry and I play together. It has never been, and I am sure never will be, my ambition to build the biggest bank balance in the world. I don't think that way, and my parents don't think that way.

However, having said all that, a person's earnings are a definite means of judging success. And, let's be honest, it's nice to know you are completely secure financially.

John Courage eased me in with a pro-am ten-pin bowling tournament they were sponsoring in Leeds. I knew as much about ten-pin bowling as Barry knows about screw-backs, so it was just as well that Steve Neff, the American number one, was flown over to partner me. Before I could even pick up a ball, Steve had to run through the rules in detail and worked overtime in getting my throwing action right.

I learnt fast. In my very first game I scored a marvellous 157. Just seven behind my coach!

'You're a Goddam hustler,' he called out.

Having started so well, I then made the terrible mistake of trying much harder, and suddenly found I couldn't hit a double-decker bus! Just as in snooker, when someone is playing badly and starts to try a lot harder, he usually goes from bad to worse. He puts too much pressure on himself, and that is fatal.

Steve Neff excelled himself and virtually achieved on the alleyway what I had achieved on the snooker table just a few weeks earlier. Eleven strikes out of twelve brought him a colossal 265 points, just thirty-five short of the maximum.

With Steve dominating the tournament, and me keeping score, we powered on to win the first prize of £1,000 each, although singer Patti Boulaye knocked me flat when beating me with one of her gentle trundles in the very last game. All in all, I thoroughly enjoyed myself, even if I did ruin my thumb!

From ten-pin bowling, my talents stretched even farther a week or two later when I was crowned Arcade Player of the Year, in a competition run by a national magazine. The final stages began with three of the country's best video players competing on The Defender, the Pac-Man and an Asteroid. The best of these three then had to meet me in the final on a brand-new machine which neither of us was supposed to have seen before.

However, while taking part in the Lada, someone had put this very machine in my dressing-room and I must have played on it a hundred times. Against such experience, the lad had little chance, although he did go home with £1,000-worth of video equipment as a consolation prize!

Explosions of a more serious kind went off at the Black Lion Sports Centre in Gillingham when Alex Higgins failed to appear for an evening's exhibition match with me. Barry went berserk and tried to telephone Geoff Lomas, a member of the Sportsworld team, the people who managed Higgins.

'Can you give me Higgins's home number?' Barry sharply asked the assistant at Potter's Snooker Club. 'I want him urgently!'

Back came the reply: 'You can speak to him now if you like. He's playing on table one!'

Barry said to Higgins, 'What are you doing up there? You should be down in Gillingham playing for me.' Higgins apologised and said that he knew nothing about the Gillingham match.

Desperately short of time, Barry arranged for amateur Russell Jarmak to play me over nine frames. Many people stayed behind to watch us but there was still a lot of bad feeling in the room, even though every customer received a full refund.

Barry later learned that Higgins had been given an itinerary. Then Sportsworld and Higgins started to blame each other for the mix-up. Barry was not satisfied that he had been told the full story, but he eventually reached a financial settlement with Higgins which included a full replacement show. And this time Alex did turn up – forty-five minutes late!

For me, the beautiful Benson and Hedges Masters trophy was the one missing piece in my major tournament jigsaw. Even as a teenager, I followed the event with envious eyes and can remember vividly being one of the excited thousands who saw Doug Mountjoy beat Ray Reardon in a most emotional final at the New London Theatre in Drury Lane in 1977. I can also remember Barry being even more excited. He had put £40 on Mountjoy at 66–1!

I particularly wanted to win the Benson because it oozes prestige, is staged in the most luxurious venue possible, the Wembley Conference Centre, is the only serious snooker tournament held in the capital, and is played in front of crowds well in excess of two thousand. Put that lot together and I think you will understand why the adrenalin begins to pump once the Masters comes in sight.

On this occasion, I started at the quarter-final stage by meeting Doug Mountjoy, which gave us yet another opportunity to relive the world championship final all over again. Doug had just abandoned his two-piece cue and switched back to a single-piece one. He felt the two-piece cue was not as good as the one which helped him win the Masters and the United Kingdom championships back in the seventies. The new cue looks a lot like his old one, but he was still getting used to it when he played me, and he was not at his best. I won in a canter by five frames to two.

Doug's special party piece is singing 'Danny Boy'. He is one of the few Welsh people I know who can actually sing. After his rendering, he usually falls asleep, much to the delight of Dennis Taylor who loves to balance the craziest objects on Doug's flat head. On one occasion, he balanced a pint of beer for fully thirty seconds, and Doug slept right through it all without moving a muscle. Dennis also likes to slip knives and spoons into Doug's pockets, especially if he takes a nap in the lounge of a crowded hotel. You could strip Doug naked on a park bench and he'd sleep on without a care in the world.

Having beaten Doug, I then went out to face Tony Meo in the semi-final, undoubtedly the most important match for me since Barry had taken over managing Tony. It was vital that I should still treat Tony as a dangerous opponent and not ease up simply because he now came from the same camp. To prove that my attitude hadn't changed, I think I played some of my best snooker to go five frames in front, hardly missing a ball.

Then, as sometimes happens to all players in big matches, I just couldn't complete the job and win the last frame. I let him off the hook, and he suddenly started to play well. Before I could gather my senses, the score was 5–4. I was struggling to hit the ball straight, and Tony was playing just as brilliantly as I had been earlier. I kept myself together in the crisis with a few small breaks and then eventually scrambled into the final with quite a scare.

Yet again, just as in the United Kingdom championships and in the Lada, the sporting Terry Griffiths was there, eagerly waiting to begin yet another quality game of snooker between the undisputed numbers one and two in the world.

A tremendous cheer from a crowd of 2,800 fanatics greeted me when I walked into the arena. The welcome was as good as I've ever had. My regular supporters didn't have to open their mouths.

By now, I was determined to win the competition, and when I dashed 6–3 in front it seemed as though I was pulling away, just as I had done in the United Kingdom final. But Terry is a great grafter and rather than me draw away, it was he who fought back, and I began to hit the ball appallingly. Crisis point came at 6–5, and looking sure to go 6–6. But then, with four reds still left on the table, I made one of the best clearances of my life, and this cracked him completely. He didn't hit another ball in a straight line.

A crisis point occurs in most matches. It's the key moment when one player must assert his authority on the game or be doomed to die. To prove I was equipped for such a test, I took the next three frames to win the match convincingly by nine frames to five. Of all my many crisis points, the one I remember best concerned Cliff Thorburn in the 1981 world championships when I returned a different person after the interval and turned a 6–8 deficit into a 16–10 victory. Of course, it is much easier to fold when a crisis comes up. It is no longer just the player's basic skills that are on trial, but more his strength of character and his will to survive.

After receiving the magnificent gold cup, a garland of flowers was placed around my neck. I felt more like a Grand Prix driver than a snooker champion.

14

Threats on the Phone

A week before the Benson, I was sitting in Barry's office when the telephone rang and a man with a North Country accent asked to speak to me. I don't usually accept calls at Romford, but we were having such a good day that I made an exception and asked him what he wanted. He began by congratulating me on my 147 break and then, in the same breath, said that the next time I went to the North, he would break my fingers.

'Oh, lovely!' I said, and put the receiver down.

I can't say he frightened me, but I was definitely a bit shocked at first. We all know that if someone is seriously thinking of hurting someone else, he doesn't usually pick up a phone and pass on a warning, but we also know that there are plenty of nutters around, and you can never be sure that it's just a hoax.

To be honest, I didn't give this nutter one more thought and simply regarded the call as nothing more than a one-off incident. What I didn't know was that he was telephoning Romford every day before the Benson. Some days he rang as many as ten times, and always repeated his threat to snap my fingers, naming the Wembley Conference Centre as the place where I would be 'looked after'.

I first began to suspect that something odd was going on when Barry and our two resident minders, drivers and caddies, Robbo and

Radley, turned up at every session dressed in large overcoats, like undertakers, and with strange-looking bulges in their pockets.

Not one of them seemed at ease, and Barry, in particular, was sweating blood in the heat of the auditorium. Time and again he was asked about putting his coat in the cloakroom, but he kept saying no – and now I know why!

The funniest moment came when I got up to visit the toilet during an interval in my match with Mountjoy. As soon as I said I was off to spend a penny, Robbo and Radley immediately jumped to their feet and said together, 'And so am I!' I just cracked up and demanded to know the full story. Barry then spilled out the lot and everyone of us stayed on full alert.

In fact, this extra pressure paid dividends for me. I suddenly felt involved in a new battle and I concentrated even harder on every shot I played.

The nutter rang again after the Benson, and Barry told him: 'Whoever you are, Steve would like to thank you very much for spurring him on. It was just the nudge he needed.' Actually the chap has become such a regular caller now that when he doesn't ring we tend to miss him. We worry that he might be seriously ill or that he's fallen under a bus. He's become part of the team.

For a while we wondered how he always knew where I was due to play. Then we realised he was getting details of my itinerary through the post by way of the *Daily Star*, who send it out to all members of my fan club. And when you've got fans like that, who needs enemies?

A short time later we took no chances again when I visited Gateshead as part of a three-man England team, aided and abetted by Tony Meo and John Virgo, to play the usual Welsh trio of Reardon, Griffiths and Mountjoy.

Ron Radley's coat was still bulging as he drove me through the night, straight from an exhibition match in Surrey where I had taken a few extra drinks to help me sleep in the car. The nightcap worked wonders. I dozed off near Watford and didn't wake up again until a few miles from my hotel in Newcastle.

We booked in at six and I slept until 10.30, rising for a lunch-time session in a match that slowly but surely became nothing more than a scrambling shambles. There was no atmosphere, no MC, and no crowd-control. All in all, it was pathetically organised.

Any match with no proper MC, will always struggle to get off the ground. Players find it impossible to raise the necessary interest to treat a match seriously unless someone is at hand to set the scene for them. If snooker is to maintain the high standard of presentation it has achieved on television, all organisers and promoters must make a big effort to stage their shows in a colourful way so that the audience and the players can feel excited by the occasion. Snooker can never receive too much razamataz, whether for an exhibition match or an international event.

With everything going so well for me on the tournament circuit, I began to concentrate harder on my financial affairs and, with the New Year coming in, I thought it was a good time to take stock. First and foremost I am a snooker player, so where cash is concerned I rely entirely on expert advice, most of it coming from my manager, friend and business partner, Barry Hearn.

When it comes to commercial matters, Barry is tremendously clever. I admire him enormously. And there is no limit to the trust I put in him. We have worked so hard together over the past five years, that I am sure we were fated to end in the position in which we now find ourselves.

Having already formed three companies to consolidate our snooker interests – Steve Davis Limited, Steve Davis Promotions Limited and Steve Davis Properties Limited – we felt the time was now right to organise ourselves even more effectively, using the same professional attitude as I do on the snooker table. Such expert advice can only come from the very best people in their own particular field. We appointed top accountants Thomas McLintock as our auditors and tax consultants; County Bank as our merchant bankers; and City solicitors, Blyth, Dutton, Holloway as our legal back-up team.

It was also right to look on the black side – just in case! So term insurance, accident and sickness insurance, life assurance, pension schemes and Unit Trust investments all followed in a succession of meetings with some of the most skilled people in the world of commerce. I was determined to obtain the right protection to ensure that my new-found wealth should not be squandered or taken away.

Barry, of course, was in his element with all this financial planning. He was already financially independent himself, so he had the experience to put together a package which left me very satisfied that I was achieving more than just success on the snooker table. These financial comings and goings were always great fun. I enjoyed meeting the experts, having lunches at bankers' offices or at the Stock Exchange, and even the endless medicals. I must have filled enough sample bottles to launch the QE2!

With all the basic details attended to, my companies were able to expand deeper into the promotional side of snooker, and I also began to take an interest in longer-term investments in property and even forestry.

The forestry deal was entirely new and appealed to me a lot. At first I thought the Steve Davis cues could come direct from the wood grown in the Steve Davis forest in the West of Scotland. However, I now understand that I could be dead and buried before the wood is ready for such commercial use. The forest itself is still growing at a rapid rate of four inches every year!

Thank goodness, because of my success and all these investments I am not likely to worry about money for the rest of my life. I have reached the stage where I play in competitions and often don't know what prizes have been put up. I have never played for money, anyway. Money should never be the main incentive for a player to do well. For me, money means that I can now go into a restaurant and not be concerned about the price of King Prawns, or whether I should order two veg instead of one.

Spending sprees don't attract me. Tapes, and some records of my favourite music are about the only items I buy regularly – apart from clothes, of course. More recently I have splashed out a little on a few video films and I shall probably go on collecting them in the same way as some people collect foreign stamps. This means that when I feel like looking at a particular film, I can take it off the shelf. It's a small luxury which I think I have earned.

After the Benson, I went to play three exhibition matches at the St Mellion Golf and Country Club in Cornwall. Barry, Susan and Tony Meo also came along. Barry's sister owns a pub in nearby Camelford and I rather overdrank my welcome.

Barry played me at darts for £50 and, after taking all afternoon to come down from 501, we both needed double-one to get out. Eric Bristow is definitely not in our class!

Later on that day, with my snooker match against Tony standing at 1–1, we agreed on a sidestake of £200 going to the winner of the decider. To my horror, when I got to the table, the whole room spun around, and after two shots I said, 'Give him the money. I can't see straight!' I sobered up on orange juice and even made a century break. But it was all too late. I had lost the match. It was unlike me to drink so much, and I went to bed vowing never to touch a drop of alcohol before a game again.

My preparation was very different for the Tolly Cobbold Classic in Ipswich. I fancied winning that one. Jimmy White and Tony Meo seemed my main obstacles, but by the time I entered the competition proper both of them had been knocked out. Jimmy crashed against Dennis Taylor, and Tony lost to Graham Miles, which I found much more of a surprise.

I started well by toppling Willie Thorne 3–0 and then beat Graham Miles 3–2, which included two big breaks that he could do nothing about. In one of them I knocked up 105 in just seven minutes. This win puts me in the 15-frame final against Dennis Taylor, who had disposed of Tony Knowles in the other semi.

I made a brilliant start and thought it must be one of those days when I had walked through a cowfield. My touch was spot-on and I led 6–0 at the interval.

Ravenously hungry, I left the arena and sat down for a huge meal at my hotel – and soon suffered for it. When I returned to the table I was carrying a 10lb penalty. I was slow and sluggish, and Dennis promptly won three of the next four frames, though I don't wish to take any credit away from him because he battled hard. As time went on I picked up again and won the Classic 8–3, earning myself an early night for a change.

I had eaten big meals during match intervals before and never suffered any after-effects, although I did once hear a doctor say that a substantial meal just before a game can slow sportsmen down, both physically and mentally. In some cases, of course, this could be advantageous, particularly if a player tends to be over-active or highly-strung.

As for myself, I can handle pressure. I don't need any outside help to slow me down. I try to play all my shots at the same pace, using a steady, even rhythm. Erratic players like Higgins and Stevens tend to fluctuate from shot to shot. One slow, one fast. There is no real tempo to their play, so their consistency is bound to suffer, and this shows up in their results.

Still, I have now decided that I shall never eat another big meal before, or during, a match again. Instead, I shall rely on just a small snack to keep the engine ticking over, the type of spartan diet I found so successful during the 1981 world championships, even if I did lose half a stone in the process.

15

An Earthquake at the Yamaha

Given the chance to choose my eventual successor as world champion, I think a ten-year-old lad from Blackburn would be high on my list. He's already a Steve Davis in miniature. He's even ginger! The lad won a local newspaper competition, and the penalty for his skill was a one-frame confrontation with me in front of a packed audience in the town hall. He had obviously watched me on television because he never laughed or joked. I bet he hadn't slept for a week thinking about the game.

When we shook hands, he got a marvellous reception. Most of all, I knew that it was vitally important that I should not deliberately leave the balls over the holes for him to pot, because when he genuinely knocked one in, he wouldn't get the applause he deserved. In fact, he played one tremendous long-pot and the crowd went wild.

I was most impressed with his performance, although some people grumbled because I didn't let him win. But that would have been farcical and unfair to the lad – and the game might have gone on for ever! I preferred to treat him with respect, and if he had beaten me, then that really would have been the biggest upset in snooker history. The lad wore a smart dinner-suit, and I couldn't help noticing that he was far better dressed than the three amateur players I faced later on in the evening.

The standard of performance among young players is definitely on the increase. I just wonder how much higher it can go in the next ten years. What, indeed, is the actual limit? In athletics we are able to measure improvement on the watch. At one time the four-minute mile was considered something of a miracle. Now it is 3 minutes 47.33 seconds. On top of that, a cricketer can hit centuries, a golfer can go round in fewer shots, and a boxer can keep knocking opponents out. Progress in those sports can be gauged with clear statistical proof. Snooker cannot be measured so precisely.

When I came along I was regarded as a perfectionist and compared with the great Joe Davis. But, basically, it is all a matter of opinion. There are no positive facts and figures on which to form a proper comparison. In time, no doubt, some other winner will appear, and the talk will be, 'Would he have beaten Steve Davis?'

All that I hope is in the very distant future. I have no intention yet of being knocked off my pedestal. I would like to think I could be up there on top for another ten years – world champion or not. My aim is simply to win more tournaments than any other player and that, I am sure, is all about consistency.

Everyone should realise that to reach the top in any sport requires sacrifices of all sorts. Most of all, time has to be found for practice. But, with so many counter-attractions around these days, young people, in particular, seem to find it difficult to discipline themselves in order to put in the hard work and dedication that are necessary to improve their game.

John Parrott, a young player from Liverpool, might be a name to put in your notebook. I saw him play when I appeared on the television programme, Sportswatch. He wasn't entirely new to me, as Frank Callen, a shrewd snooker judge, had praised him highly as a promising teenager.

I went on the programme chiefly to demonstrate the trick-shot of my choice. I picked the machine-gun one and made a right hash of it! To achieve this trick, I place seven balls in a line across the table, roll the white ball towards the corner pocket, and then fire each of the seven balls rapidly towards the same pocket, hoping beyond hope that they will all go in before the white one goes down. Hence the term 'machine-gun'.

It took me forty-five minutes to play the shot well, and even then I didn't get it right. The producer finally settled for my best effort, but the white ball was still resting on the lip, having refused to drop. Thanks to the power of taped television, viewers probably thought it was my first shot, and counted me a bit unlucky, yet in truth it must have been my twentieth. In artificial conditions like that it is often impossible to achieve those targets that come quite easily in normal circumstances, as I found to my horror when making the television commercials.

Though I was defending the Yamaha Organs title, and extremely keen to keep the crown, my feelings on entering the event were nowhere near as exciting as when I prepared for the Benson.

The Yamaha format was terribly complicated, and we all know that anything that is difficult to understand usually ends up by confusing people. The promoters decided that every match up to the semi-final stage should be played over the best-of-three frames on a round-robin basis. In those circumstances, I knew I could hardly be slated if I went out early.

All I can say in favour of this format is that it gave the spectators a chance to see four players in action on the same day, rather than the usual two. But it still didn't appeal to me. It also put instant pressure on the players. Not one of us could afford to drop a frame, and this naturally created even more excitement for those in the crowd.

Of course, luck was bound to play a big part. But even then it was still Terry Griffiths and I who came through to fight out the finish. This again seemed to suggest that no matter how much luck is involved in a tournament, class will tell in the end. Perhaps it is further proof that the best players usually come out on top because they can handle pressure so much better than those lower down.

To reach the final I encountered my fair share of scares, none more nasty than when I slumped against Ray Edmonds – a national disaster that almost held up the nine o'clock news. The media went wild about it.

Before that shock, I had started off well. I had dismissed Bill Werbeniuk 2–0 by freezing him out with some confident snooker, so all I had to do was beat Edmonds to guarantee myself a place in the semi-final group. On form, no bookmaker in the world could bet against me. Though an experienced professional for many years, Ray is not strictly rated among the world's top ten, and is certainly not someone I regard as a dangerous opponent. But snooker earthquakes do occur from time to time and suddenly Edmonds was showing 2–1 on the Richter Scale.

It was a ridiculous turnabout. Only minutes earlier I had monopolised our first frame, winning by a massive 132 points to nil, but a silly mistake in our next game meant I lost command and he went on to win the match in great style.

Ray and I shared the same dressing-room and when we arrived back there, he went to his coat and took out a small Whiff cigar. Then he smiled at me, put it down, and said, 'Oh, hell, it's time to celebrate!' And he pulled a much larger one from his pocket.

Having lost to Ray, I now had to beat Kirk Stevens to be sure of qualifying for the semi-final group. Kirk blew a fairly easy chance in the first frame, and from then on the match was mine and I had no problem in ending up top of my group. John Virgo, Dennis Taylor and Edmonds joined me in the semi-final, and I was determined that Edmonds should not beat me again.

My first game, against Virgo, eventually proved to be the most important of them all. I beat him 2–0 and although I went on to win the rest of my games, it was Virgo who kept closest to me, ending up second in the group.

I enjoyed a day's rest before the final and waited to see who came through from the other group. I didn't exactly fall off my seat when I heard it was Terry Griffiths.

The final proved to be one of the best matches we have ever played against each other. The skill and tactics were of the highest calibre and many people later complimented us both on the way we played.

Enjoying a good start, I took a 4–1 lead. Terry levelled at 4–4, and then I stayed in front up to 8–7, when it seemed certain it would go to 8–8. But completely out of the blue I produced one of the best clearances of my life and made sure that the trophy remained with me in Romford.

As I had started to play the piano, it seemed appropriate that I should also record the tournament's highest break to win a beautiful portable organ which I now take with me everywhere. Neat and compact, it fits easily into my Porsche, though it's a bit more difficult to play than my old harmonica as I drive up and down the motorways!

Even before I won it, I had bought an identical organ direct from

Making the news with Jan Leeming as Pye Personalities of the Year.

Waiting in the wings. Embassy World Championships, 1982.

I'm 8–1 down and the writing's on the wall.

The party's over, but I'll be back.

The pride of Romford. Terry, Tony, me, Barry and Vic.

A royal occasion . . . Princess Michael of Kent, Susan, Barry and me.

Possibly the world's worst referee. Frank Mizzlebrook in attentive pose.

'Seriously, Mizz, you're terrific, but why do you keep re-spotting the reds?'

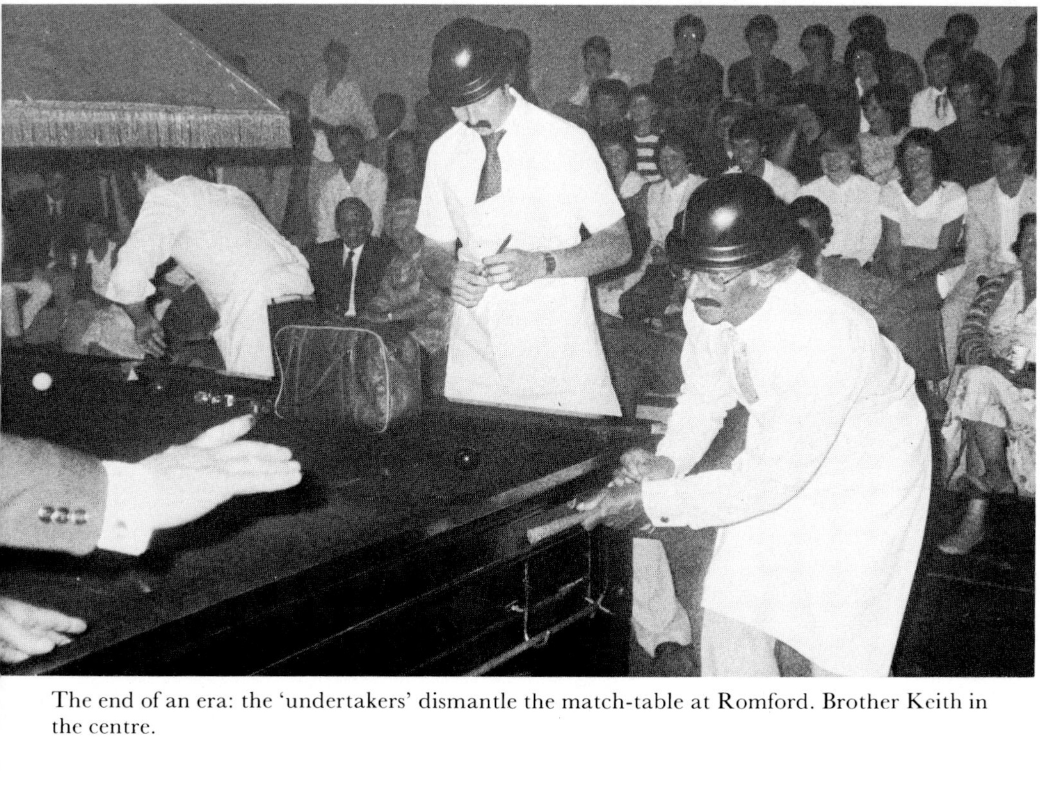

The end of an era: the 'undertakers' dismantle the match-table at Romford. Brother Keith in the centre.

Win or lose, my number one fan. My mum, Jean.

Yamaha. Not having enough fingers to play two, I passed the spare one to Barry's wife Susan, and we are now enjoying a private competition to see who can play 'Ba-Ba Black Sheep' first.

Yamaha also sold me a baby-grand piano, but when it arrived at my parents' home in Plumstead we found it was too big for the front room, so it was put in cold storage while dad knocked down a few walls and built a new staircase. We had often talked of altering the house, but who could have thought it would have been forced on us by a baby-grand – and me as the pianist?

Before playing in the Yamaha, a representative of Granada Television asked if I would allow a film crew to live with me right through the world championships, to put together a fly-on-the-wall documentary. Barry and I said no to this, even though the man lined up for the job had won two world awards for documentary programmes. We thought a film crew in those circumstances would come too close to me and get under my skin. We had learnt our lesson when a girl reporter from a national newspaper travelled with me for a week and was hardly discreet in what she wrote.

A camera lens stuck in your lap, poked over your shoulder and under your chin, day in, day out, for any length of time can make it impossible for even the most placid person to be himself. All championships produce a type of pressure that is beyond explaining, and it is certainly not the time or place to have people looking in and seeing the strain you are under. This is the time when peace and privacy are at a premium, so I am sure we made the right decision. To Granada's credit, though, producer Paul Docherty sent me a great telegram after I won the Yamaha which said, 'Well done, champ! So what was your problem?'

It was shortly after the Yamaha that I literally lost the World Cup. I put it down in a Bristol hotel and calmly drove off without it.

By a remarkable coincidence, Paul Hatherell, of Snookasport Promotions, the company who run the world championships, and who lives in Bristol, happened to walk into the same hotel and couldn't believe his eyes when he saw the cup.

Straightaway he telephoned Barry and pretended he wanted the cup to be sent for engraving. At first, Barry gasped, 'Oh, hell, where is it?' Then he realised there was no point in bluffing and confessed that I had left it in Bristol.

'I know,' said Paul. 'I've just sent it off to be engraved.'

Altogether the trophy was out of my hands for seven days. Then I lost it again in Sheffield a few weeks later. This time Alex Higgins picked it up, and promised to look after it for twelve months for me!

16

Pursued by a Sex Maniac

News of the close encounters between Terry and me excited them so much in the Isle of Man that when we arrived for a nine-frame exhibition match we found that the show was not just a sell-out, but that a video system had been installed to pipe the game into a discotheque next door. I felt more like a boxer than a snooker player.

Arriving back in London, I stepped straight into a double-dose of Noel Edmunds. First on television, then on radio. On his television show, Swap Shop, I left myself wide open for a few giggles when I agreed to read out a number of swaps that had been deliberately laced with a variety of double meanings.

Next day, I again took the mike, this time making history by playing the first-ever snooker match on the radio. A table was placed in an adjoining studio and the idea was for Noel and me to play a frame of snooker over the air, with a commentator at hand to give a shot-by-shot account of what was happening.

Because the sound wouldn't go out loudly enough from a boom microphone suspended over the table, small microphones were clipped to our sweaters and we walked around the room like dogs on leads, with the ends plugged into a wall. It caused a great laugh, because we couldn't move around the table without crossing each other's path and tying ourselves in knots.

The pockets were so tight that we could hardly pot a ball, and some of those listening must have thought it was all a practical joke. Several people came up to me later and asked whether we really did have a table to play on.

I then made the mistake of saying I would like to be a disc-jockey for a day, and Noel promptly handed me a motoring report. The typist I'm afraid had lost a finger and left out a 'W'. So instead of saying Wokingham, I read out Okingham and caused traffic jams all over the country as baffled motorists dived for their maps.

Hardly an exhibition match goes by without a good laugh of some sort, but none could compare with the evening Barry and I spent raising funds at the Clayberry Mental Hospital in Essex.

Two women officers met us at the door, along with a man we thought was a member of the staff. He greeted us by offering the back of his left hand, which we thought was odd, though we didn't comment on it at the time.

Before playing the exhibition match proper, I agreed to play a fun frame in the elderly ward against one of the patients. But the man who had practised for a month to take me on now couldn't get out of his chair through nerves.

Another patient played in his place, and when he potted a good black I went up to him and said, 'Well done.' But he turned his back on me and walked away. I kept talking to him through the game, but he never replied.

'Funny fellow,' I thought. It was only much later that someone told me he was stone deaf!

By now I had noticed that the man who met us at the door was strolling up and down the corridor, winking at us, singing, and with a weird look in his eye. I asked a staff nurse who he was, and she said quietly, 'He's a sex maniac. He attacks girls.' One of his favourite pastimes was buying a packet of crisps, tipping the salt down a nurse's blouse and then trying to retrieve it.

I went to Barry and told him a sex maniac was on the loose, and Barry said, 'What the hell was he doing, meeting us at the door? People like that should be locked up. Where has he come from?'

'He's probably escaped from B Ward,' said the nurse. 'They'll find him in an hour or two!'

Patients in the old people's ward had baked a huge cake for me and put iced music notes around the sides, and a small plastic piano on the top. A fruit cake, no less! The sex maniac walked up to the table to cut the cake, picked up the knife and kept looking at it, staring at it, in a trance. He was remarkably polite, but he kept looking 'through' everyone.

The staff tried to take photographs of me, but he kept standing in the front and wanted to be in them all. He also wanted to follow me to the exhibition match proper – but was detained on the way, thank God! In most cases the patients looked so normal that I had trouble separating them from the staff, though this chap gave me no problems. I was sure I had seen him in *One Flew Over the Cuckoo's Nest.*

My grand tour of the mental homes continued a week later when I played for charity at the Warley Hospital, again in Essex, and included a number of trick shots in my programme.

For one of them, I placed the black ball in the jaws of a bottom pocket and then proceeded to pot it with a 10p piece which I cued along the cushion, the full length of the table.

Before I played the shot, I placed the white ball well away from the action and, as it's part of my usual patter, I said without thinking, 'All those lunatics in the audience might wonder why the white ball is down the other side of the table. . . .' As soon as the word lunatic left my lips, I went stone cold. It was the most embarrassing moment of my life.

To finish off my programme, I thanked patients and staff for providing my lunch and said that I would go anywhere for a free meal. To which the patients replied, 'Well, come inside, silly Steve' – and set off a roar of weird laughter right across the room.

A certain amount of insanity crept into the Irish Benson and Hedges Masters a short time later, when Higgins blew a gasket while playing me in the semi-final.

'Keep your mouths shut,' he shouted to his fans, and referee John Smyth, himself an Irishman, stepped in and warned Higgins that he could disqualify him. Higgins was obviously frustrated because he wasn't playing as well against me as he would have liked in front of his own people. I managed to beat him fairly easily 6–2 and the remark cost him £1,000 and a good ticking off from the Players' Association for bringing the game into disrepute.

Earlier on, while beating Doug Mountjoy, I put together a 128 clearance, which stood right through as the tournament's highest break.

Surprise, surprise, it was Terry Griffiths who again came through to play me in the final. Though not keyed up for the competition in the same way as I am for most of the other big tournaments, I was still keen to win. By now, Terry had virtually made the title his own and was trying to take it home for the third year in a row.

As it turned out, I raced into a 3–0 lead and was coasting. It seemed that Terry's reign was over. But the Welsh king doesn't abdicate that easily. He rallied, went in front, and kept his crown.

On reflection, I was probably too complacent. I allowed him to come back when he should have been frozen out. I was very disappointed at the way I played. I left there thinking it was a timely reminder for me, with the world championships coming up, that I had to work a lot harder at my game, and not to be over-confident about it.

I am sure that it is more than coincidence that the two best players in the world have a regular band of supporters who would go to the Falklands to watch them play.

In the same way as Barry attends most of my matches, Terry's good friend Peter Francis is rarely far away when he is playing. The same applies to my dad and to Terry's dad. Both of them are always present at major tournaments to share the traumas with us.

I can't think of one other player who enjoys the same type of loyal and personal support. It is always there when we need it most – when we are under the severest pressure. When we win, of course, they are as thrilled as we are, and when we lose, it hurts them just as much as it hurts us. Our disappointment is their disappointment. Personal feelings of this sort extend far beyond the table and provide enormous encouragement and inspiration, although it is always down to the player in the end.

Unless a heatwave hits Great Yarmouth in the next few years, I'm going to be sticking around there for some time. I am to stand in the seaside waxworks, which I regard as a nice compliment, although I I am not looking forward to seeing myself all greased up like death. It all started when a man rang up and said he wanted to measure my head. Before I could choke him off he quickly explained that it was only to get the size right for the wax model. A spate of photographs then followed, with the camera clicking at all angles to make sure the rest of me was in exact proportion.

When I think of all the occasions that I am asked to turn up to please my public, and many of them at short notice, I am amazed that I arrive for them all, and almost always on time. One that did go slightly wrong involved a school prize-giving close to my home. It astounds me that I could get to Sydney on time, yet managed to mess up a meeting just five hundred yards from my front door.

A headmaster had telephoned Barry and asked if I could attend a prize-giving at my old school. When Barry told me, I automatically assumed it was my senior school, Abbey Wood Comprehensive. I arrived on time, but the headmaster gave me a puzzled look and said, 'We had our prize-giving a week ago, but as you're here, why not take a quick tour of your old classrooms?'

Meanwhile, back at Barry's office, a panicking headmaster from my junior school, the Alexandra McLeod, had telephoned to say that he had five hundred kids wondering what had happened to me. Barry passed the message on, and I dashed around the corner just in time to hand out the prizes.

I first began to think seriously of the world championships as many as three to four weeks before my opening match against Tony Knowles on 29 April. Even with the championships closing on me so rapidly, I saw no reason to ease up on my schedule. Keeping on the move meant I had less time to dwell on the task of defending my title.

Barry quite deliberately mixed up my preparation with exhibition matches, plenty of practice, a tournament in Scotland, book-signings and a great day relaxing at golf in a John Courage event in Southampton. Cannon and Ball, two of the funniest men in showbusiness, also put me in a marvellous mood with a truly classic sketch in which I played a frame of snooker on an invisible table for a £50 bet, using sound effects for the click of the balls.

The Courage golf day, extravagantly called the Steve Davis Classic, came to a riotous finish. Robbo caddied for Barry, and Ronnie Radley caddied for me. Robbo was under the strictest instructions not to take fresh balls from his bag and drop them in favourable places for Barry to gain an advantage. Earlier in the year Robbo had been reported for doing just that to help Barry in a pro-am tournament.

As long as I beat Barry I don't care about my standard of play, and Barry feels exactly the same way about me. But we do treat winning seriously, and I wouldn't advise anyone of the Christian faith to follow us around, for fear of choking on the blue air we tend to generate.

As usual our play at Southampton was far from brilliant, but the ribbing between us exceeded everything that had gone on before. By the fourteenth we were all-square, and there was so much banter flying around about who would win that Barry suddenly decided he wanted a £50 bet.

To me, there is nothing worse than losing. Win at all costs, that's my motto, provided you don't have to cheat. And anyone who argues differently will never be a winner as long as he lives.

On reaching the seventeenth, Barry had gone two shots in front. He had fired impressively since the lager started to flow at the ninth, our stopping-off point. When it comes to drink, it must be said that Barry can hold it a lot better than I can.

We both played two shots to the seventeenth and I was getting down for my third when a television crew burst from the bushes and started to film us. Immediately I saw the cameras I thought, 'Great! Great! I'm good on TV,' and played a fantastic pitch shot, sending the ball close to the hole.

Then all of a sudden the cameras were focused on Barry, and the pressure was much too great for him. A large chunk of turf flew high towards the seventeenth – with the ball still lying on the ground! His next shot was no better, the ball trickling ten yards from his feet.

On leaving the seventeenth, we were level. And while we teed up for our drives to the last hole the cameras were still buzzing on all sides of us. Barry played first and again fluffed his shot. This let me in for a glorious surge to the last green and, though I had the luxury of three shots to win, I needed only two of them.

TV South used the film as a news item and promised to send me a copy. Barry made it plain he didn't want one! So the day I beat my manager at golf is now recorded on tape for all time, and should shut him up for good.

From Southampton I drove straight to Scotland for the Highland Masters at Inverness. If I could have altered anything about my programme at this time, perhaps I would have missed out this tournament and concentrated more on practice.

Still, it was not all work. I took a few hours off and went roller-skating with friends. Another entirely new experience that was rather painful in the end! I wasn't keen to try it at first, thinking I might break a few bones and hobble to Sheffield on crutches. Considering the way I played, I don't suppose they would have made much difference.

As time went by, I realised I couldn't wrap myself in cotton wool for ever, so I stuck my feet in a pair of skates and looked a right lemon. I tried to move on two feet, but I couldn't move on one! The rink manager saw my predicament and came up and said quietly, 'Mr Davis, would you like to pop upstairs for a quick lesson from our coach?'

'Delighted!' I said, and almost kissed him.

I crawled up the stairs, still wearing my skates, and the coach said, 'First of all we must make sure you can go round the corners.' After forty-five minutes he had taught me how to negotiate corners and was praising my ability to learn quickly, even though I was still falling over regularly.

'I think you are ready to go back downstairs now,' he said, smiling optimistically.

The madding throng were going round in large circles, which I thought was made for me – until I realised the coach hadn't told me how to skate in a straight line. Absolutely baffled, I ended up going round and round in ever-decreasing circles until I found myself stranded in the middle, struggling to get off the rink. I lost count of the times I fell, and I could hardly walk. My left hip was black and blue, and killing me. It was great fun!

The Highland Masters was just as traumatic. Playing in front of small crowds, and with no atmosphere, I struggled to beat Matt Gibson 4–3 in the quarter-final after trailing 3–2, and then crashed out 6–0 to Ray Reardon in the semi-final. Alex Higgins also lost 6–0, to John Spencer in the other semi, so who could possibly have predicted that in a matter of days Higgins would be beating Reardon in a stirring final to become the new world champion?

Obviously I was professionally aware of playing badly – as badly as I'd ever done. The rot had set in and I had lost a little confidence, which I was trying desperately hard to recover. But I wasn't too worried, because I thought that when the real incentive came along my game would pick up automatically.

I had no worries about my technique. I felt my cue action was as sound as ever, my stance was right and I was playing at my normal speed. My father, one of my sternest critics on technique, hadn't complained, so I couldn't have been doing a lot wrong in that department.

Deep down, I feel it is impossible for any sportsman to be at his peak every time he takes up a new challenge. Lapses of concentration are bound to occur, errors are unavoidable. It's all part of being human. Just as snooker players miss pots, footballers miss goals, golfers miss putts, and cricketers miss the ball. We snooker players are slightly worse off than other sportsmen because in most major tournaments the cameras are breathing down our necks all the time and applying even greater pressure.

From Scotland, I drove straight to Trentham Gardens, near Birmingham, to play Terry Griffiths in a much-publicised £5,000 winner-take-all match over nine frames. Terry won it 5–3.

Though neither of us was brilliant, Terry proved the stronger. After seeing so much of him at this time, and particularly the way he played in Ireland, I couldn't realistically think of any other player who could give me the slightest problem in the world championships.

17
Cooked at the Crucible

Despite having just lost to Reardon and Terry, and definitely going through a slump, I didn't expect any trouble from Tony Knowles in my first-round match at Sheffield. There was nothing in the form-book to make me think otherwise.

With four to five days left before the championships, I knew my form had returned and I started to play well, Having worried professionally about whether I could drag myself out of the rut in time, I was now pleased with the way I was striking the ball.

Ironically, a few days before the championships, Letts published my technical book, *Successful Snooker*, and after Tony Knowles had beaten me, I joked that I ought to go back and read it from cover to cover.

To launch the book I attended signing sessions in London, Manchester, Birmingham and Sheffield, and I was very pleased with the large numbers of people who came along. Some critics tried to say that signing sessions like those contributed to my loss of form. I couldn't think of anything more unlikely. I enjoy sitting in a chair chatting to people, which can hardly be described as hard work. If people were honest I'm sure they would all say that it's a nice part of life to be the centre of attraction.

It was raining when I left my hotel to play my first-round match against Tony, and Barry called a taxi. Being superstitious, Barry was bothered because it meant we couldn't now follow the 'lucky' route he mapped out for me around the streets of Sheffield the previous year. In particular, it meant we couldn't jump on the wooden dray doors outside the pub a hundred yards from The Crucible.

Before going into the match with Tony, I warmed up for half an hour on the practice table backstage, alongside the temporary television studio where David Vine did his interviews. I was now hitting the ball as sweetly as I'd ever done, and was confident of playing well.

Of course, returning to Sheffield to defend my title brought with it a new type of pressure. Not least, being reminded constantly that no champion had ever successfully defended his crown there.

At no time, from the day the draw was made, did I look forward to playing Tony. There was no incentive in it for me. If I had gone out to play someone who had proved himself, like Reardon, Griffiths or Higgins, I think I would have been ready for battle and raised my game. But I took it for granted that I would beat Tony, although I was experienced enough to know that once I reached the table I couldn't afford to be complacent.

Looking at the draw, I decided my first tough match would be in the semi-finals against John Virgo or Reardon. I prepared myself mentally for a struggle at that stage, and no earlier. So when Tony stormed in at me, I wasn't mentally keyed up for him. Tony is a good player with lots of potential, but nothing he had achieved up to then could seriously suggest that he would give me the slightest trouble, let alone beat me 10–1.

Some newspapers, and even one or two players, said that I was worn out. That I had spent too much time playing in exhibition matches, travelling, and being a celebrity. They thought I should have taken a long rest and come up fresh. Rubbish! Terry Griffiths did that, and look what happened to him. He went no farther than I did.

I was perfectly happy with my preparation. I was satisfied that I had practised as thoroughly as I had done the previous year. At the same time, I can't deny that I worked hard at exhibition matches and on promotional engagements, but then I enjoyed them all and didn't find them a drag. I like meeting people and, as world champion, I felt I had a basic duty to find time to go out and mix with the public.

There was no single, simple explanation for my exit. It was more a combination of little problems that built up into a huge monster to make the match a living hell for me.

First and foremost, it never crossed my mind that Tony could beat me. That was the biggest mistake of all, and it taught me a lesson I shall never forget. On paper, it looked a pushover, but he soon changed all that. I had told myself from time to time that I should not underestimate him, but when I compared our individual records I couldn't realistically regard him as a serious threat.

Secondly, I was playing so badly so close to the championships that my confidence had been sapped, and though I began to hit the ball well a few days before my match, my form had returned too late. I suppose my enthusiasm to fulfil public demands didn't help, either. It meant I didn't give myself enough time to be alone to relax and think clearly. I was a bit of a toy soldier, all wound up, with the spring getting tighter and tighter.

Also, having to play in the first match of the championships meant that my adrenalin was far from pumping. I was like a fish being taken from cold water and thrown into hot water. I think every player will agree that it takes at least two to three days before the real championship bug begins to bite and you start to feel the excitement boiling in your blood.

On reflection, I might have gone in too cool. I had no nerves about me. I didn't shake or panic, and never once felt pressure although, of course, I was under extreme pressure because the ball certainly didn't run kindly for me. I went out to play in the same frame of mind as when I lost to Perrie Mans in the Benson and Hedges the previous year. I was unable to assess the table quickly enough. I had to think harder. Very little came naturally. I wasn't exactly helpless, but just slow and almost in a daze.

I kept asking myself, 'What shall I do here? What can I do now?' Normally I would have seen the next shot straightaway and played it confidently. I was definitely not tuned in.

Right up to 6–1, I just laughed at my luck. I kept waiting for the bad 'run' to stop so that I could work my way into the game. Then I sensed that it wasn't going to stop, and I knew I was on my way out.

I wasn't exactly happy with the table, either. It was definitely one of the most difficult I have played on. It was built differently from the ones I am used to, especially the cushions, which were supported by steel strips rather than the more conventional wooden ones. This caused the ball to bounce off more sharply than I was accustomed to. The pockets were also tight and, believe me, there is nothing worse, when you are struggling to get into a game, than playing on a strange table with tight pockets. For the first time Bristol Coin were allowed to install their table, as opposed to the Riley table used in most tournaments and about which I had been so complimentary in the 1981 world championships.

When I left The Crucible that Friday night, I was trailing 8–1. I refused to be despondent and went straight to my hotel and ate a huge steak, washed it down with a glass of champagne, and enjoyed a great laugh with Barry and a few friends from Romford. Barry summed up the situation when he ordered the champagne and announced to our entourage, 'We normally drink this at the end of a successful tournament, so rather than wait, we'll drink it now!'

Even then, with Tony needing just two frames to clinch the match next morning, I accepted that there could be no miracle fightback, and I virtually conceded defeat.

This was an entirely new experience for me. I had never before been in a position where disaster came on the first day of a major tournament, so I made the most of it – and drank a few lagers, as well!

Being philosophical, I told myself to look forward. To dismiss it all as a bad dream. I vowed that I would be much harder in future, that I would seize my opportunities, and that I would not allow one isolated slip to cause me the slightest worry. I knew this defeat would make me a harder competitor, would strengthen my professional character and would help prepare me for the time when I would return to The Crucible to try again for the title.

Basically, the defeat will not make the slightest difference to me as a person or change my style as a player. Why should it? People are still coming up and saying that all I did was miss out on one tournament in a fantastic season. They keep referring to my successes in the Jameson, the Coral UK, the Benson and Hedges Masters, the Yamaha Classic, Pontin's and television's *Pot Black*. And just about all of them have said that it is this type of consistency that makes a worthy champion.

Looked at in those terms, I suppose I ended the year winning 6–1 against all-comers, so there can't be too much wrong with my standard of play. On top of my tournament wins, I also claimed a sweet piece of history with the first televised 147 break, and at a time when I was mentally and physically down on my knees after a frantic, sleepless trip around the world.

Every player in the game is experienced enough to understand that the world champion need not necessarily be the best player in the world. And since the championships, several people have pointed out that in tennis and golf there is no recognised world champion, and that in motor racing, for example, the world championship is decided on by a points system based on a series of Grand Prix races run over several months. At times – like the moment I was trailing Tony 8–1 – I feel snooker could do with a similar points system and, who knows, it might reflect more accurately the standard of performance over a whole season, rather than have it judged on the result of a single event, which can be terribly misleading. No one could argue then that one win doesn't make a champion!

Three video machines were brought into my hotel to help me relax through the championship fortnight. Don Tate soon mastered one of them, while I tried to learn a bit about them both. Shortly after losing to Tony, I went to the video-room to wind down and said to Don, 'Well, what are you going to challenge me on?' Quick as a flash, he replied, 'Snooker!'

With my cue put back in its case, Terry Griffiths became the obvious new favourite. But even more shocks were in store, and his stay was no longer than mine. Willie Thorne, playing some of his best snooker, which included the championship's highest break of 143, killed him off by ten frames to six, which, for many people, immediately reduced the competition to little more than a guessing-game.

With Willie in action, it became clear that pressure can build up not only at the table, but from the Press, as well. I feel sure he must have suffered from a large piece of smut that one newspaper printed about his past domestic life. It was only news because he was doing well in the championships, and wouldn't have made a line at any other time. I genuinely felt for him. I knew how much pressure he was under in the game without having this load of rubbish to contend with. Only he knows how much it upset him, but he battled on bravely until going out to Higgins 13–10.

As for Terry, I think he might have felt certain for some time that he would be in the final against me, and a lot of other people thought the same. So when I went out, the pressure automatically switched to him. On all the form he had shown in the weeks leading up to the championships, he had every right to think that the title was now virtually in his grasp.

With Terry also knocked out, the critics finally gave me a rest and stopped trying to work out where I had gone wrong. All of a sudden, the competition was thrown into confusion and uncertainty. With the first two favourites no longer in the fight, the event took on a strange new feeling.

I like to think that between us, Terry and I have raised the level of the game. I also like to think that we are excellent ambassadors, not only for snooker itself, but for sport in general. Young people in particular will always look up to a champion, so it is vitally important that whoever reaches the top and sits on the throne, should set the very best example, not only as a performer, but in the way he conducts himself outside the arena.

Despite the way the championships ended, with Reardon and Higgins reaching the final, I still believe that Jimmy White is the only player, apart from Terry and myself, who can raise his game to a high level and keep it there for any reasonable length of time.

On performances over the year, I was number-one and Terry was number-two. Not even Higgins could dispute that. It will now be interesting to see whether Higgins, who beat Reardon 18–15, can prove that he's capable of winning, not just one tournament, but others as well.

As a whole, I think the championships failed to reach the standard many people expected, probably because the pockets were so tight, which tended to level out performances.

Regarding individual efforts, Tony Knowles obviously proved he has now matured a great deal and, having beaten me, his confidence must have soared sky high. It may also give him just the encouragement he needs to begin to believe in his own ability.

Dean Reynolds was an interesting newcomer. Though I have yet to see him in a match, I did catch a glimpse of his technique on the practice table. He's not the most natural player in the world – certainly not as natural as Jimmy White – but he still pots the balls, and that's what the game is all about.

Dean, it seems, had a raw deal from referee John Williams in his match against South Africa's big man, Silvino Fransisco. John Williams warned Dean for allegedly playing too slowly, a decision many people thought both harsh and unfair. Having made a number of mistakes and survived in his opening match against Fred Davis, the absolute master of gamesmanship, it was asking a lot of Dean to cope with the referee's pressure, as well. To his credit, Dean did well to shrug off the warning, although the more experienced Silvino eventually beat him in the end.

One television commentator timed the frames John Williams complained about and noted that not one of them lasted more than thirty minutes. On this occasion, there seems little doubt that John was a trifle hard on a lad so young, and on someone who was making his début in the heat of the world championships. As for Silvino, well he's a veteran campaigner by now, and I can't envisage any great opportunities suddenly opening up for him. He went out to Ray Reardon in the quarter-finals.

Tony Knowles plugged on with remarkable confidence, reached the quarter-finals, and took a massive lead against Eddie Charlton. With Tony on top by ten frames to six, and needing only three frames for a semi-final shot, it would have taken a brave man to bet against him.

But Charlton is an experienced battler. He's not easily rattled. He maintains a calm, steady pace no matter how the game is going.

This was no different. Keeping cool, he began to produce some fine shots and Tony suddenly went to pieces. All the confidence and natural rhythm that had featured so strongly in his play up to then, totally deserted him. Gradually, shot by shot, frame by frame, Charlton clawed his way back, crept ahead, and took the match by thirteen frames to eleven.

Tony must have kicked himself for letting such a fantastic chance slip through his fingers. If he had beaten Charlton – and he should have – I'm sure he could have gone on and beaten Reardon and found himself in the final.

As it turned out, Reardon proved much too strong for Charlton, reeling off five frames in a row to win 16–11 and become a finalist for the first time since 1978, when he beat Perrie Mans for his sixth title. Reardon had never lost in a final. He had definitely played well in the weeks before the championships and produced flashes of his old vintage years, but overall he was still quite short of the form that he consistently produced during his heyday.

The game's two undisputed speed kings, Alex Higgins and Jimmy White met in the other semi-final, an electrifying clash which many people thought would have been better as the final. When you look closely at each player, Higgins is seen as slightly cleverer than Jimmy. He's more cagey. And it was probably this slight superiority in safety play which won Higgins a match that will long be remembered for Jimmy's potting and for Alex's incredible clearance when defeat seemed inevitable.

Higgins's great escape came in frame thirty. Jimmy led 15–14, was 59–0 up, and it looked curtains for Alex. But he refused to lie down, unleashed some tremendous snooker and took the frame with a glorious clearance of 69. Higgins was now in full flight. Unstoppable. And he took the final frame 96–16.

I have no wish to criticise Jimmy, but he threw away a magnificent chance to become the youngest player ever to appear in a world championship final. One bad miss was enough to let Higgins in. If Jimmy had sunk that last simple red and extended his 59–0 lead, there was no way in which Higgins could have come back into the game.

Jimmy misses like that because he plays every shot at the same pace. He is faster into his shots than Higgins. The trouble is, he never takes into account the state of the game. Some shots require a more sedate approach, a little more care. They might not be more difficult in potting terms, but the state of the game might demand more caution.

But Jimmy always wants to get on with the show. He has no time to breathe. It all boils down to instinct and self-preservation, but it must still be regarded as a flaw in his game. A mental flaw rather than a technical one. Of course, he's just made that way. I doubt whether he could change even if he wanted to. It's all part of his personality. A part of the style and flair that combine to make Jimmy so brilliant and so different from other players.

Reardon versus Higgins made for a good final, although the Reardon of a year ago could never have stood up to him. I even thought that Reardon could win, mainly because he is one of the few players Higgins genuinely respects. Higgins tends to treat most players with mild contempt. There are just a few whom he truly respects, and I think I can count myself as one of them.

Reardon hadn't won a major tournament for four years, so that alone underlined the way in which he had prepared for these championships. However, he faltered in the closing stages and Higgins went from strength to strength. He finished off with a truly brilliant 135 clearance, and never looked like missing a ball, to take the title 18–15.

I looked at him closely before that last frame and I could tell by the expression on his face that he knew the title was his, and that he was longing to explode and produce something special right at the end for everyone to remember him by.

Looking closely at the way Higgins won, I definitely believe he was helped by having to play in the harder half of the draw. I was in the harder half the previous year, and it certainly helped me. Being in the tougher section means you remain keyed up. There is no time to relax or become complacent. Every match is virtually a final.

I also think Higgins was fated to win. I know the type of person he is, and as soon as Terry and I were knocked out, he would regard that as an omen. We were the only two he would genuinely fear.

On seeing the last ball go down, Higgins burst into tears and was very emotional, especially for a man who is renowned for playing it hard. The moment he saw his baby girl in the crowd, he really cracked. He had said for days that she was his driving force, and once she was brought up to him at the table, he found it impossible to keep back the tears.

I know the feeling well. It is very real. There is nothing superficial about it. After two weeks of being under so much pressure, with your mental stamina stretched to the limit, it is impossible not to show emotion when the championships are all over and you've come out on top. I defy anyone to say that Alex and I were putting it on. If anyone thinks that, then he can't begin to grasp what it means to be a world champion.

The only other time I got so close to tears was when I made the 147. As soon as I saw everyone standing up and cheering, I realised how much it meant to me and to them, and I felt my eyes misting up. I also imagined it going out on television and being seen by millions. I had made history, and I felt proud of being part of something big.

Actually the emotion tends to swell whenever I accomplish a 'first'. It happened with my first UK win, my first Benson and Hedges and when I led England in the world team championships.

In a way, this was a 'first' for Alex, too, Though he won the world title in 1972, the championships have become a lot more important since then. They are now as much a part of the sporting calendar as Wimbledon or the Open golf.

I have also experienced tears of a different kind. Not for a first, but for a 'last'.

18

The Machine is Repaired

Shortly after the championships, Barry decided to revamp the match-room at Romford where I spent endless hours in my youth playing and practising, and where my career took off.

To mark the end of an era, Barry laid on one of his special parties for all those people close to us, and he and I played the very last frame in the room before six mechanics, all dressed up as undertakers, came through the doors and proceeded to take the table apart piece by piece. It was a very emotional moment for me. It was a bit like losing a friend, and there was no way in which I could keep my eyes dry.

On being knocked out of the championships, I went home for a few days and called at the local supermarket where I once worked as a lad. The till-girl I had a crush on at the time was still there, but she didn't remember me.

While I was in the store, I signed a few autographs for people and thought it odd when a woman came along with a young girl who seemed to be hanging back. All was made clear when the woman said, 'Would you please sign your book for my daughter – and could you write it out to Toni Knowles?'

During those few days at home, I awoke one morning to find that my car had been broken into and a few things stolen. I wouldn't have been so upset, except that whoever was responsible took all my cassettes, and didn't fancy my posters or my life-story book!

I suppose one of the nice things about being successful in sport is that you come in for all those wonderful perks other people just dream about. One of these pleasant occasions came when I was invited to the John Courage 'farewell' party to the England soccer squad before they flew out to Spain for the World Cup finals. A class at the Bannockburn School in Plumstead, where my mother teaches, had drawn pictures of the team, and I passed them on as good luck charms. In return, Ron Greenwood handed me a soccer ball signed by all twenty-two players, and I took it back for the children to drool over.

Just two days after the championships, I was booked to play Alex in a nine-frame exhibition match at Warrington, a game the Press inevitably built up into a showdown between the new king and his predecessor. One reporter wrote: 'The match is billed as an exhibition, but when Davis meets Higgins, well, we all know better....' That summed it up perfectly.

In one respect I would have fancied a short holiday, but I knew it was vitally important that I should prove to everyone that losing at Sheffield was nothing more than an unpleasant hiccup. My record against Higgins is particularly good, so deep down inside I welcomed this opportunity to challenge him so soon after the championships.

As you'd expect, the match was an early sell-out. I have never seen so many reporters and Press cameras in attendance, even at major tournaments. The place just tingled with excitement.

In the two days between winning the title and coming to play in that match, Higgins had been fined £1,000 by snooker's governing body for bringing the game into disrepute. It was the heaviest penalty ever imposed by the World Professional Billiards and Snooker Association. The offence mainly concerned Higgins's 'shut your mouth' outburst to his fans while playing me in Dublin, but it also took into account his much-publicised watering of a Crucible flower-pot.

In such a great atmosphere I would have loved to be sitting up in the commentators' box and taken the liberty of saying, 'Alex took a right slash at that plant!' In fact, shortly after the championships, John Virgo was doing his impersonation act at Pontin's when he put his cue on the table, dashed to a flower-pot in true Higgins fashion, cocked his leg and pretended to saturate the plants. It brought the house down.

I was determined to do well at Warrington and I beat him 5–1. We met again the next night, this time at Wythenshawe near Manchester, right in the heart of Higgins's home ground. Unfortunately, the match eventually received as much Press coverage for the crowd's appalling behaviour as it did for the snooker.

Those who caused the trouble were a small group of noisy Higgins supporters. No one can enjoy playing in front of such ignorant people, and it's no secret that we all prefer to play for sensible supporters rather than hysterical or drunken ones. The few ignorant people kept shouting out and making it clear whose side they were on, even cheering when I missed a shot and went in-off.

Yet, for all those who supported Higgins, I was not entirely on my own. One brave woman kept shouting out, 'Come on, Stevie, do your stuff!' At one stage, I played a very slow red, and as the ball got closer and closer to the hole, a few of the unbiased spectators bawled out, 'Miss! Miss!' Obviously frustrated that I was not getting enough support, the woman stood up, turned on the noisy rabble and shouted out even louder, 'Why don't you shut your faces!' For the rest of that frame, I just couldn't stop laughing. In the third frame, I put together a break of 96, the highest of the evening, so she did, at least, have something to cheer about.

Half-way through the match she came up and complained that referee John Williams had warned her to keep quiet, but had not warned anyone else. I was not surprised. If John Williams had warned the others there was a real danger he would have been carried out with a dart in his head.

Though I don't enjoy playing in such a bad atmosphere, I have come to regard that type of conduct as a back-handed compliment. I no longer get upset if people clap when I go in-off. If they want me to lose that badly, and they think it's the only way possible, then I must consider it as a poorly disguised compliment. It makes me feel good, although the noise itself can be terribly distracting.

From the time I turned professional I quickly came to terms with the fact that it didn't matter how many people liked me – there would always be those who would hate me.

It applies to other players, too. It's a fact of life. Some people just can't bear to see other people doing well.

From the din of Wythenshawe, I went straight to Southend for a two-day Barry Hearn–Steve Davis promotion, playing Terry Griffiths in front of television cameras in the £7,000 Courage Challenge on the Friday, and playing two further matches against Higgins on the Saturday.

Again it was extremely important that I should do well. The Griffiths match was being screened next day for seventeen million viewers as part of a large Cup Final programme. A prize of £7,000 was on offer, but all I cared about was winning. I'm sure Terry felt the same. With such a huge national audience, it was a golden opportunity to re-establish ourselves in the public eye. Though the snooker was never spectacular, I beat him 5–3, and that's all that mattered to me. I did the job.

Both my Saturday matches against Higgins were absolute sell-outs. This was a big compliment to snooker, bearing in mind that the Cup Final was being shown live on both channels. I beat Alex 5–1 in the afternoon, and 5–3 in the evening. The snooker often reached a very high standard, with several big breaks, including an impeccable 143 from Higgins, and a 116 clearance by myself. The crowd enjoyed the games so much that they kept asking me when we were going back to resume our battles.

I was seeing a great deal of Higgins at this stage, and it was quite noticeable that he was far less obnoxious since winning the title. Obviously, this made for a much better atmosphere between us, and I just hoped that he would stay that way and not slip back into his bad habits.

Extremely encouraged by the way I played at Southend, I drove to Pontin's next day with my mind firmly set on winning the professional event for the very first time. I beat Willie Thorne 6–3, Doug Mountjoy 7–3 and found myself in the final against Ray Reardon. Brimming with confidence, I dashed into a 4–0 lead, before Reardon picked himself up and drew level at 4–4. I went ahead again in the next frame, and we looked like going to 5–5 when I produced one of the best shots I have ever played in a match.

We were all square on points, and just the pink and black were left on the table. The pink was placed just outside the 'D', with the white ball close to the cushion, down the other end of the table, and almost in line with the pink spot.

Though I had virtually a direct shot to the bottom left-hand corner pocket, I also had the enormous problem of how to strike the cue-ball in order to gain good position on the black. For a moment I thought it might be better to play a safety shot, but I decided to take a calculated risk and go for the pot. This meant I had to attempt what seemed an impossible screw-back. I had to raise the cue almost to a vertical position and then dig down hard on the cue-ball itself.

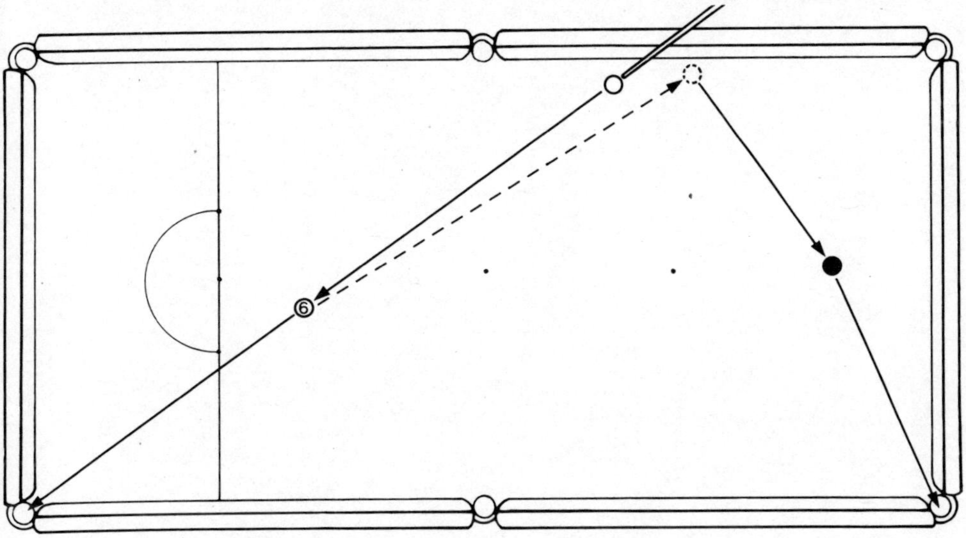

The shot in the Pontin's Professional that I shall never forget–a deep screw-back on the pink in the final against Ray Reardon.

To my amazement the pink flew in and I achieved the perfect screw-back, finishing directly behind the black and in a straight line to the corner pocket. My only problem now was that I was back tight on the cushion and with very little room in which to attack the cue-ball again.

I steadied myself, played confidently, and the black went down. Many people told me later that the pink was one of the best shots they had ever seen struck by any player. For my own part, I couldn't remember playing a better one at any stage of my life.

Though the £3,500 prize was not big by current snooker standards, it was very important that I should secure yet another title for the year, and end the season on a winning note. At this point the world championships were barely a fortnight past and I had already played both finalists and beaten them comprehensively.

If nothing else, it made me feel good. It proved that losing my title had been quickly forgotten, was totally out of my system and, most important of all, that I had recovered my enormous appetite for the wonderful game of snooker.

I was in no doubt that the machine had been repaired.

Appendix

Steve Davis's 1981–2 season

1981

SEPTEMBER:

Jameson International Open (Derby)

Beat: Perrie Mans 5–3
David Taylor 5–1
Alex Higgins 9–8
Dennis Taylor 9–0 (final).

OCTOBER:

Laing Scottish Masters (Glasgow)

Lost to Jimmy White 6–5 (semi-final)

NOVEMBER:

State Express world team championships (Reading)

England (David Taylor, John Spencer and Steve Davis) beat *Wales* (Ray Reardon, Terry Griffiths, Doug Mountjoy) 4–3 in final.

DECEMBER:

Coral UK championships (Preston)

Beat: Willie Thorne 9–2
Bill Werbeniuk 9–5
Jimmy White 9–0
Terry Griffiths 16–3 (final).

BBC Sports Personality of the Year: Runner-up to Ian Botham

Filmed TV Christmas Show with Eric Morecambe and Ernie Wise

Pro-celebrity tournament (Leeds). Partnered Frankie Vaughan

1982

JANUARY:

Lada Classic (Oldham)

Lost to Terry Griffiths, on black, 9–8 (final).

Made history – achieved first 147 break on television.

Visited Sydney and Las Vegas to promote snooker tournaments.

Benson and Hedges Masters (Wembley)

Beat: Terry Griffiths 9–5 (final).

FEBRUARY:

Tolly Cobbold Classic (Ipswich)

Beat: Dennis Taylor 8–3 (final).

MARCH:

Pot Black (Birmingham). Filmed in December

Beat: Eddie Charlton 2–0 (final).

Yamaha Organs International (Derby)

Beat: Terry Griffiths 9–7 (final).

Irish Benson and Hedges Masters

Lost to Terry Griffiths 9–5 (final).

Filmed with Cannon and Ball.

APRIL:

Highland Masters

Lost to Ray Reardon 6–0 (semi-final).

Trentham Challenge Match

Lost to Terry Griffiths 5–3.

World championships (Sheffield)

Lost to Tony Knowles 10–1.

MAY:

Pontin's Professional (Prestatyn)

Beat: Ray Reardon 9–4 (final).

John Courage Challenge (Southend)

Beat: Terry Griffiths 5–3.